Book 3 of Tools for Lightworkers Series

I0225311

Opening Quantum Doorways

Prayers of Intent
&
Guided Visualizations

Lorelynn Mirage Cardo, Ph.D.

Copyright

Author:
Lorelynn Mirage Cardo
www.ariseguide.com

Book Layout, Interior Design, and Production:
Cue Raven Publishing
www.cueravenpublishing.com

Illustrations:
Kristin Broten
www.kristinbrotenart.com

Publisher:
Arise Enterprises, LLC
Lorelynn Mirage Cardo, PhD.

1st Edition

ISBN 13: 978-0-9980113-3-2
ISBN 10:

Library of Congress:

Table of Contents

Introduction

This is the 3rd book of the Tools for Lightworkers series and I am so honored to offer this book to you!

Over the years I have been asked by many clients, students and apprentices to provide more information and instruction on these two vital areas of energy healing. I encourage you to enjoy the adventure of walking through gateways and dimensions to your own sacred spaces, dialoguing with Spirit and setting intent for yourself, your healings, and to those people and situations you are drawn.

I have written this book for those who are serious about becoming a healer and, especially, for those who wish to increase their healing and empowering work as Lightworkers.

Are you a Lightworker? If you are reading this, you are!

What is a Lightworker? A Lightworker is someone who chooses light over darkness, who chooses hope over despair, who chooses forgiveness and understanding over revenge, brittleness, and hardenings, and who chooses tolerance and compassion over judgment, apathy and cruelty. As I've said, if you are reading this, trust you Are a Lightworker!

Prayers of Intent are important focal points for energy healers in every situation. Prayers of Intent help your client but, most importantly, they help you step along a dimensional pathway, bringing clarity and consciousness to your daily life. It opens you to sacred space and to an access into Unified Consciousness.

The same is true for Guided Visualizations. They are designed to help your client in a healing session or energy course relax, deepen, and, if it is their choice, to step through a quantum doorway into sacred, multidimensional space where anything and Anyone is possible. Just as importantly, Guided Visualizations help you navigate through dimensions, increase your higher gifts, and more easily access higher information.

By becoming more comfortable and familiar with Prayers of Intent and Guided Visualizations, as Lightworkers, we are able to light up every day in every way!

EnJoy!

Part 1

Standing

at the Brink

of

Infinity

Introduction

Understanding who we are, what time we live in, and what gifts we have built- in all form an essential backdrop to everything we do as energy healers. These understandings are also important for the design and potency of both Prayers of Intent and Guided Visualizations.

Without this foundation in place, or, at least re-examined, you will be dancing between worlds, spiraling through faith and hope that your work is true -- and anxiety and doubt that your work is illusionary.

In Prayers of Intent and Guided Visualizations do we open quantum portals and enter multidimensional space? Yes.

Do you need to believe that *you* are able to open portals and enter multidimensional space? No.

Like a placebo effect, belief can help but is not necessary.

Is it easier, more authentic, and humbling- yet- exhilarating if you clear up knotty spaces inside yourself and then step forward to do this work? Yes! Definitely.

Personal, direct experience is the better teacher and verifier than belief alone.

Because, really, why can't you open quantum portals and enter multidimensional space?

Who taught you that you couldn't?

In the following three chapters, we cover the basics of opening quantum portals and entering multidimensional space. We, truly, are *Standing at the Brink of Infinity*. Let yourself expand into this reality. The first chapter, Quantum Jumps, covers the nature of reality as you understand it to be. Sounds philosophical, but it is essential. The second chapter, Quantum Connections, covers the Guests we invoke to partner with us in our work. Both of these chapters cover your subconscious, conscious and superconscious filters.

Let's get started!

Chapter 1

Quantum Jumps
Evolution of Consciousness

There are hundreds of years here and there where history books tell us life was bucolic, settled, and fairly peaceful. These are not our descriptors! We live in uncertain, murky, and quickly shifting times!

Visualize a large, slowly moving river and throw a stone in. Watch the splash and the concentric circles which radiate outwards until the original river flow resumes. Now, throw in a 2nd rock and watch the action. Again, jaunty splashes! You will also notice the concentric waves of the second stone interfere with the rhythm of the first.

Throw in a 3rd stone. Sit back and watch the bobbling, interweaving patterns, cresting playfully, perhaps uncovering some debris from the depths. The waters churn in a state of flux, trying to assimilate and integrate the immersions and interference waves. Finally, add a 4th rock into the churning, patterned mix. Hard to even see the patterns, waves, circles.

This is a metaphor for the times we are living in right now.

We stand at the brink of four large rocks which have been thrown into the river of our reality. And, the rocks are large, more like boulders! What patterns can we see? What do our eyes behold?

As a young child, I liked to lay on my bed and look out my window from different perspectives. It seemed surprising that when I closed my right eye, I saw one view of the window and fire escape metal bars. Then, when I closed the left eye, I saw a different view. I opened both eyes – and the fire escape and window pane merged into one unified vision. I practiced this for a long time, trying to understand what I was seeing. Why did it look differently with an eye closed?

Let's try closing one eye and viewing this river scene above with the rock splashes and the resulting interference wave patterns.

Monovision:
Throwing God-Sized Boulders in the Current of Time

Let's try an experiment together. As I closed one eye at a time to look at the perspective of the fire escape, we will close one eye to view the history of our consensual reality and view two quantum jumps. One is through the lens of child of nature and the other is child of God. Monovision shows us each viewpoint.

Quantum Jump 1: Child of Nature

Let's imagine that we are viewing from on-high, a singular vision of the first rock thrown into our collective consciousness. The first rock was thrown in tens of thousands, perhaps hundreds of thousands of years ago. This first wave is comprised of super-natural, divinely ordained, origin stories and myths about the nature of reality, the nature of life on earth, and the reason for human life. Elders' beliefs were handed down as realities, generation after generation.

Humankind developed from an earth and sky-based understanding of Deities, communicating comfortably with the Divine and with the elements.

There was a sense of a wholeness of consciousness and a communal survival mechanism that we have lost through the millennia. Matriarchal, indigenous, earth honoring systems abounded. There was a sense of being one with the earth, one with the group. The overarching ethos might be:

> *"We survive, or we die, together."*

> *"We live in an abundant system; our Mother provides all."*

In the evolution of our consensus global consciousness, there are subtle, faint glimpses of these ancient concentric circles rippling from this one-with-nature, man as child-of-nature worldview. Modern-day Shamans and Indigenous Elders are working to bring back this forgotten perspective and tool kit. For most of us, this is a dream state.

Quantum Jump 2: Child of God

The next boulder thrown into the river of time made waves that overwhelmed and integrated the concentric circles from those first rocks and it is still forming tsunami-sized cresting waves in our consciousness today. This is the boulder of Monotheism. The pantheistic and Goddess oriented societies eventually gave way to patriarchal, or male dominated power systems. The rise of individual imperative over the common good became the global operating system and this has been in effect for the previous five to ten thousand years.

We believed in our God, who was the only right God. God created everything we see around us, and our place became as 'children of God'. This monovision moved humankind from child-of-nature to child-of-God. Jews, Christians, Muslims, all believe in the same basic scriptures and God lineage – and yet each tribe's perception of the One True God is something that has been fought over and died over for thousands of years, with no end yet in sight.

Within this system there has been the rise of global religious hierarchies and worldviews. Within this One God ethos, there are still the overarching super-natural, Divinely created and inspired origin stories which give humanity a sense of shelter in the storm of infinity.

There is an overriding sense of mission and purpose in this worldview, although the individual person is cut off from Mother Nature and remains at the mercy of, or the child of, an authoritarian parent and externally based rule books. The rise of monotheism devolved into a cry of:

"My God is better than your God."

"My way is right, yours is wrong."

Roman Catholicism, the merging of proto-Christianity with the Roman military and hierarchical machinery, held tight reins on prevailing thought, culture, and views of what is real, what is unreal, what is possible, what is impossible. Within the Christian tradition, the consensus reality was that we are born sinners and, therefore, it was necessary for Christ to die for us and our sins so that we can live, forever, in heaven. Where this particular belief came from is an interesting thread, but outside the scope of this book (hint, economic and power structures).

This structured perception of reality lasted through crucifixions, crusades, inquisitions, and cobbled thinking up until the Protestant Reformation. This 'reforming' did break the constructs of papal and 'infallible' influence, yet, Protesting Christianity retained the monotheistic, sinner archetype, and the necessity for an intermediary between man and (a judging) God.

History is replete with examples repeated, over and over again, of differing God tribes conquering each other, changing the religious landscape, bringing their worldview, or else. Sacred texts all say that man is created in the image of God, but, it can also be said that God is also made in the image of man. God is presented through the lens of the conjoined consciousness of the people and culture of that time period.

We know abuses and rigidities occurred. Protestant religions formed in protest to the abuses of Catholic priests selling indulgences, or special passes, which got wealthy people directly into heaven, regardless of their actions or intents.

This wave, Child-of-God consciousness is still washing over us daily, with every political and geopolitical news story. According to the Pew Research Center, the following is the approximate global religious population:

2.5 billion	Christian (including 1.3 billion Catholics)
1.7 billion	Islam
1.2 billion	Non-Religious*
1 billion	Hindu
500 million	Buddhist
400 million	Folk religions (including African, Chinese, Native American & Aborigine)
58 million	Other religions (including Sikhism, Shintoism, Jainism, Baha'i, Taoism, Zoroastrianism, etc.)
20 million	Judaism

*'Non-religious' comes in at number 3 globally. This includes those who answer surveys as indifferent, rejecting, or hostile to religions.

As we are still very much swimming and keeping afloat in the waves of this global consensus reality, it is good to take a moment before moving forward and answer for yourself some of these questions. They might be part of your subconscious, conscious or super-conscious landscapes. It is important as we develop the Lightworker tools of Prayer of Intent and Guided Visualizations to know what your underpinnings are. You might want to re-file, rename, or re-frame some of them.

Who are you?

Why are you here?

Where are you going?

Where have your loved ones gone?

Will we live forever?

What does timeless eternity mean?

What were you taught?

What do you believe is real?

What are you not sure of?

Do you believe your way is the only way?

And, as Christianity is the largest religion on the planet at this time, consider the following Christian-based precepts:

Are we children?

Is God a father?

Do we have a mother?

Are we born sinners?

Why are we born sinners?

Are we subject to pain and suffering because Eve ate an apple?

The stranglehold of religious thought on newly burgeoning 'experimental scientists' became strained to its ultimate endpoint, when the next large boulder was thrown into our space-time continuum.

Binocular Vision:
Calculating Mass and Velocity of a New Boulder

Let us continue with our vision experiment. Instead of looking out the window of my Flushing, Queens apartment at the bars of the fire escape with one eye closed, I opened both eyes to see the unified, binocular perspective. Let's use our binocular vision. We are seeing the positive space of the last wave, the Child of God, phase. We are also seeing the opposite perspective or negative space: I Am Alone.

Quantum Jump 3: I Am Alone

A tsunami of thought and consciousness has been built upon the Renaissance thinkers from the 12ᵗʰ century. As a wave, it has been building and cresting for almost one thousand years. The intellectual "Age of Enlightenment' is considered the triumph of science and philosophy (consensual reality) and it has been inexorably building from the 17ᵗʰ century. Giants such as Newton, Bacon, Descartes, Locke and others valued rationalism and a knowledge base built on experimentation. The common thread of this paradigm is an emphasis on individual rights and freedoms.

Western civilization changed forever with Newton and his clockwork mechanistic design of the universe and with Darwin and his theory of natural selection of the species. For the last 300 years, science has become our prevailing 'religion', or lens and filter of reality. It has brought about a major global shift in consciousness.

Rather than relying on beliefs handed down for generations based upon unknown or unverifiable outside sources, science makes careful and replicable observations, theories, and experiments to get at 'truth' and 'reality'. There are many assumptions which have accumulated during the last 300 years of the scientific paradigm. In his book, *Supernormal,* Dean Radin lists 8 of them:

1. Realism: Objects are completely independent of observation

2. Localism: Objects are completely separate

3. Causality: Time moves from past to future with no exception

4. Mechanism: Everything can be understood as causal networks, like gears in a clock

5. Physicalism: All statements analytically provable like logic and math can be reduced to experimentally verifiable facts

6. Materialism: Everything, including mind, is made of matter or energy. Anything else is 'immaterial' and either does not exist or is irrelevant

7. Determinism: No free will. All events are caused by preceding states

8. Reductionism: Objects are made up of a hierarchy of ever smaller objects, with subatomic at the bottom. All causation is upward, from micro to macroscopic

Most of us, entrained in the western, scientific worldview, have incorporated this thinking reflexively through our education process. Without really understanding what these underlying 8 postulates were, they were and still are not presented as worldviews or as assumptions, but as the one true reality.

The scientific viewpoint can be seen as:

"There is either no God or the whole thing is irrelevant. Only science and matter matters."

"Inner experience is irrelevant. It cannot be replicated in a laboratory. Therefore, it is not real; or, not acceptable in knowledgeable company."

"My credentials and experiments prove my way is right, yours is wrong. I am a scientist, you are ignorant and superstitious."

The scientific worldview has permeated all western culture with atheism as the accepted scientific filter of reality. Collectively, we live in a world devoid of meaning and purpose, in an unintelligent cosmos, with life hanging in the balance of random mutations. Anything else is seen as taboo, supernatural, superstitious, and ignorant.

Researchers who push the boundaries of this perceptual blockade are not physically tortured and killed these days, but their reputations and job prospects are restricted, and they are professionally humiliated and ignored. This is one strong reason that 'irreligious' has moved to number 3 in the global statistical survey of religions from the Pew Research survey, listed above.

Strange times indeed when what we personally know, through internal experience, is deemed 'irrelevant'. Only the approved (mechanistic/scientific) view is validated by the authorities or the powers that be. In the Christian era, Gnostics (or those who delved within for the experience Christ offered) were hounded and killed because the prevailing thought was that the priests told the masses what to believe and the masses believed.

In our present worldview, the scientists tell the masses what is real or not, and the masses believe, or are subject to ridicule and isolation. There are many examples of this in every discipline through the 'hard' sciences as well as the 'soft' or social sciences.

Alongside this viewpoint is the one which has evolved (smile) from Darwin's theory of natural selection. To Darwinists, the victors survive through competition, self- sufficiency, and aggression. These are primary ways to progress. Either we are at the top or we are eaten by someone at the top. And, this scientific worldview doesn't stop with biology, but has trickled down to philosophy, education, economics, and morality.

The social Darwin mindset subtexts are:

"I am 'successful', therefore, I am better than you."

"My family and I survive and thrive. You can die (you deserve to die if you can't be self-sufficient because you will pull us all down)."

"We live in a scare resource system and I win at all costs."

As a result of social Darwinism, we are very much treading water, trying not to sink, individually and collectively, along with our entire global ecosystems. We cannot see clearly through the foam and churning of the waves, to the patterns underneath it all.

We also are not clearly being told that many eminent scientists across multiple disciplines have determined this reasoning is faulty. Species survive through cooperation, partnership, and harmony. That is our way forward, although not everyone wants to walk this path of benevolence, empathy, compassion, equality and freedom.

Let's take a moment before moving forward and answer for yourself some questions. They impact everything we do as Lightworkers!

What were you taught in school about the scientific method?

What were you taught in school about natural selection?

What were you taught in school about 'survival of the fittest'?

What were you taught about the origin of the universe?

What does a 'big bang' of something from nothing really mean?

Have you talked to a scientist about your feelings of a Higher Power? How do you think they would respond?

How would an educator or 'credentialed' expert of any discipline re-act if you told them you are opening quantum doorways and setting conscious intent to affect change?

We are currently in the process of birthing a new worldview/paradigm which is quantum based. On the sub-microscopic level, things don't act like the clockwork mechanisms science has come to rely upon. Quantum experiments do not validate **any** of the above scientific assumptions!

Jumping from Binocular to Holographic Vision

Seeing is believing. Believing is seeing. We live in a Quantum Soup and we are only in year 6 of the shift in awareness.

Quantum Jump 4: Infinite Potential

A little over 100 years ago, the quantum revolution began. In earth history, it is not even a blink of an eye. And, yet, there is vast amount of data – with astonishing implications – which have been kept quiet within the secret fortress of physicists. They work in the language of mathematics, information sciences, and practical applications (technology).

Experimental results baffle scientists, and have done so for the previous 100 years, since quantum hit the waves (smile). Light photons can be waves or particles, depending upon observation. Traditional scientists view consciousness - and all personal and subjective experience! - as a brain function, if they admit to even the word, 'consciousness', at all. However, consciousness is rising – literally and metaphorically.

The implications of living in potentiality, probability, intent, and consciousness has not yet trickled down to the 'soft' sciences of psychology, sociology, economics and education. But, those of us who work in the Quantum – energy healers and Lightworkers – intuitively grasp the meaning behind the veil shrouding universal order and majesty.

If you told a physicist that, as a Lightworker and energy worker, we work within the quantum realm (I have done this), prepare yourself as they slowly back away as if the merest whiff of you will taint them forever.

One physicist I spoke with, after facing his own health crisis, designed an energy healing technique involving biology, energy healing principles, and working within the quantum. I naively assumed he would not be as (strongly and negatively) opinionated as other physicists. I was wrong. He openly stated only he could do energy work, because he was a physicist and knew mathematics. He didn't believe any of us (energy healers) could do the same, and openly sneered at us in his audience. During his 4-hour lecture on the very positive findings of his energy healing method, he took questions where he attempted to humiliate and intimidate anyone else who dared to voice their findings in the energy healing field.

Another, a world- renowned physicist, came to town for a lecture series. He insisted that, if it is true we live in multiple dimensions (something string theory insists), then the dimensions must be mathematical. The inference was that no one else except those with higher math and physics degrees can speak of (or have any personal knowledge of) these multi- dimensions. Just as certain religious groups believe they are the only ones who can access Jesus or God, certain scientists believe they are the only ones who can speak or work within the quantum. In many ways, these two seemingly opposing groups are very similar!

Their 'owning' the quantum serves to keep all of us peons at bay. If you (still) buy into the idea that only brilliant mathematicians are the keepers of the secrets of quantum – you are bringing old timey worldviews ('experts' and intermediaries) into the new consciousness.

In a quantum, holistic, aware universe there is benevolence, cooperation, probability, possibility, intelligence and creativity. Consciousness is inherent in and transcendent in everything. WE are Consciousness made flesh!

The quantum worldview broadcasts:

"We live in an intelligent universe that is full of infinite potential."

"I set conscious intent for my joy. Like unto itself is drawn."

"I envision the best for all. All is One."

Quantum Waves Breaking onto the Shore

The earliest quantum experiments showed that the very act of observing changes everything. Particles were shot through a double slit mechanism. The assumption was they would show up on the screen, after going through one or the other of the double slits, as particles. They didn't! They showed up as waves (energy, potential). However, when they were being observed, they 'behaved' and showed up as particles. There is fluid movement between matter and energy; observation (consciousness) is the key.

Russian scientists performed experiments and inserted chaotic, unrelated particles in a vacuum tube. Next, they added a single strand of DNA. The chaotic particles formed a coherent, synthesized pattern. The experimenters removed the DNA and the pattern remained for a substantial length of time. There is a template, or pattern, behind life!

There is so much more to the origins of the universe, the origins of life, and to the meaning of our lives, than random, chance, mutations. We have barely begun to peer behind the curtain of 'reality'.

How are you alive?

Why are you here?

Where did you come from?

Where will you go?

What is your belief about man's genesis? Are we descended from monkeys, God, Adam and Eve, ET intervention, some combination? Your basic worldview can give you tremendous information about your underlying filters of reality and your personal cosmology!

"I'm not sure" can be an accurate answer as we tread water carefully within these turbulent waves. We might be waiting for more confirmation from our intermediaries of reality, um, scientists. But, how do you think this unknowingness and uncertainty affects our lives when we don't know who we are or why we are here? And, why are we waiting for someone else to tell us?

Experiments have shown us our DNA holds keys to templates and coherence. It turns out we do have an instruction manual written inside! Now, we need a Quantum Rosetta Stone – aligned with our Consciousness – to read it. And, that, too, is built in.

Why wouldn't it be?

Quantum Jumps

The phrase, 'taking a quantum jump' in everyday language, means taking a sudden, huge step forward, maybe one you didn't see coming. In scientific lingo it refers to electrons and their orbital movement.

As with our previous discussion of worldviews, the movements of planets and stars were thought to be very orderly and rhythmical, even when the scientists of the times put Earth in the center and the sun and planets revolved around Earth. Everything was orderly, everyone knew their place. It was a complicated system called the 'harmony of the spheres', and, according to their data, it actually worked. Eventually, the sun became central to planetary orbits and we know that we live in a heliocentric system.

Through the electron microscope, the view of the atom seemed similar to the static solar system. The large nucleus was the 'sun', the electrons were the 'planets' spinning around their center.

In the quantum age we have entered, properties delight and confound! Electrons don't follow a stable orbit, they pop in and out of positions, and there is only a probability they will appear at a given point. They even pop in and out of existence. Quantum is about infinite potential. And, about consciousness.

In quantum jumps, we move through dimensions of here-and-now to the possibility of opening doorways and stepping through to multi-dimensions where there is no time and space as we know it. We can, therefore, theoretically, (and, in our work, practically), access Beings of Love and Light by our conscious intent. We jump. They appear. We appear. We observe. Consciousness entails. Higher Consciousness prevails.

Not only is the sky the limit – infinity is No limit!

But, is it real?

Or, are we just making all this up?

What is 'Real'?

How do we know what is real? Worldviews have changed tremendously. People believed in gods and goddesses, witches and demons, harmonic spheres circling around a central Earth, and, even recently for a few people, flat earths. People thought the Milky Way was the entirety of the universe.

Experimental Lenses of Reality

Our sense of what is real and what is not is constantly shifting and changing. 'Dark energy' and 'dark matter' are current vague and vogue descriptors of theoretically unknown energy and unknown matter, according to esteemed astrophysicists, based on current understandings of mathematical data. A few renegade scientists don't believe our mathematics are correct and are looking for other explanations of the data. The debate continues.

'Consensus reality' indicates that we all buy into a certain understanding of what is real. In earlier times, our scientists were strongly rooted in philosophy. This lasted up until the 1950's when pragmatic technologies and weaponry became more important. David Kaiser in *How the Hippies Saved Physics* details when the meaning and motives behind theoretical physics got lost. Physicists who wished to understand the implications of quantum became marginalized. We lost the meaning of quantum physics just as we lost the soul in psychology (soul = psyche). Our civilization reflects this loss of meaning and purpose in our sciences.

We are in a strong mix of waves of consensual consciousness, battling over right and wrong. The current wave, the Quantum Jump in Consciousness, although building in momentum, is still fairly young at only 100 years. It is populated by … you and me. Lightworkers. Those who are beginning to look at the world through holographic lenses, beyond monovision and binocular vision.

This worldview is also populated by some rogue scientists and academics, some ministry (Pierre de Chardin was a revolutionary in theology), and by everyday heroes. Rabble rousers who are actively fighting for global unity, tolerance, equality, and dignity for all peoples, knowing this is, and must be, the way forward. Activists who are shouting to be heard above cruelty and greed to give voice to the voiceless, including our beloved planet, Gaia, and all her creatures. Compassion in action. Those who are standing at the precipice of Co-creator conscious design, learning the workings of Law of Attraction, facing down conglomerates who try to own our health and wellness, our physical, mental and emotional integrity.

The number of people in this wave of consciousness is growing, although shame, ridicule, and ostracism are still the weapons used, in polite societies for those of us on the current edge, or, as Esther Hicks says, on the 'leading edge of thought'. In horrific regimes of all denominations, martyrdom is still occurring. Witness the breathtaking magnificence of Malala Yousafzai who stands as a present-day Joan of Arc. And, millions more are joining the chorus, sung and unsung. Including you!

The big, important questions seem not to be asked of us, ever. We might not think they matter. They do! We have been trained in specific ways how think and what to believe is 'real'. This sidesteps our responsibility for personally asking and getting answers.

Knowing that we have incarnated for this time and this purpose helps!

Knowing that we have the right and the ability to hold a larger, higher vision helps!

We Are the Filters of Reality

We perceive the world through our senses. We interpret these sense impressions as windows through the worlds of sight, sound, taste, touch, and scent. Yet, it is more accurate to say that our senses are perceptual filters that block impressions down to a tiny fraction of what exists, only letting in a minute bandwidth of information for us to process.

For example, the visible light spectrum, everything that we can see, is a fraction of the electro-magnetic spectrum. We don't see X-rays, microwave, gamma rays, infrared, radio waves. In fact, if you spread the light spectrum

25

out, it would stretch across the entire United States from NY to California. What we perceive, the visible light spectrum, would be equivalent to the size of a dime! We see 0.0035% of the light spectrum with our eyes!

If you enjoy looking at the magnificent pictures of the cosmos – like the Horsehead Nebula, the Crab Nebula, the Pillars of God, the Eye of God – understand that the universe is now visible to us because of telescopes like Hubble and Kepler which take pictures for us, outside our visible light spectrum. Without the filters allowing us to perceive the universe though various other waves, we would not see awe-inspiring photos of these celestial wonders.

The same is true for all our other senses. We filter out most of what exists. This is for optimal functioning, and for help with redundancies of information in our perceptual fields. We would get totally inundated with the amount of available information and our processing of so much information would paralyze us, grinding down our actions and choices.

Our senses aren't the only things that block our perceptions. Our minds do as well. Mind is a magnificent organic machine which filters out the vast majority of impressions, memories, thoughts so that we can focus and stay alive. When high emotions come into play, notice how you can read people and situations incorrectly, over- or underexaggerating what was said or done. It is basic human nature. Human survival training has helped us do just that – survive.

By dropping some of our limiting beliefs and perceptual filters, we are able to take in more of what is around us in our abundant world. The macroscopic and the microscopic. They are one and the same ("As above, so below"), even if our scientists, from Einstein onwards, have unsuccessfully been looking for the 'Grand Unifying Theory of Everything'. They haven't found it yet, probably because they are using shuttered filters and incomplete data; and the consensual reality must be conjoined.

Here we come, full circle, to the beginnings of a Quantum Worldview. There are quantum doorways and quantum perceptions. You will be working within them for Prayers of Intent and for Guided Visualizations. Scientists are working diligently to ensure mathematics be the primary language in this new worldview. If you don't know advanced mathematics, you are not invited to the table.

But, magnificently, it seems that consciousness is the primary mover! We all are invited! Those who understand this, experience this, and believe this, are on the cutting edge of society. A small number of scientists agree: they are again merging the implications of this quantum wave and the meaning and purpose of life. They, too, are telling us look through the lens of consciousness!

Right now, we are living in a society that is swirling and churning between worldviews. There are still many, especially indigenous tribes and shamans of all kinds, who work within the 1st (Child of Nature) worldview. There are billions who hold to the 2nd (Child of God) worldview. The majority in the western world holds firmly to the 3rd (I Am Alone) worldview.

Now, we add the 4th worldview that is advancing, gaining clarity and voice. And, unbelievably, healers and energy workers are on the forefront of this work! We may not speak the same language of scientists (mathematics as the ultimate) but, we work within this paradigm. More importantly, we live it. We watch and are humbled by the miracles which unfold daily.

Does Energy Matter?

This discussion of the nature of reality is fundamental to who you are as a person and how you live your life as a Lightworker.

Most people do not understand or take the time to realize the swirling currents they have been raised within. Some integrate only what they were taught at home. Some accept only what they were taught in school. Some feel splintered inside, believing one thing, afraid to believe another, and, even worse, afraid to experience what is there, within their bandwidth, to experience.

Because, they might (very well) be sneered at, ridiculed, shunned, talked about, made fun of, etc. Luckily, these are not 'burning times'! But, yes, you might easily be shamed and ridiculed by family, friends, colleagues, and your taunting mental loops.

Sometimes, it is hard to open ourselves to this (inner and outer) world of multidimensional delight, because it means we have to break away from social systems, which hold survival traits that have been passed down for eons. And, then, to speak one's truth to the outside world? To loved ones? Takes insight and courage indeed!

Some questions for you to consider:

Do we have the ability, and the right, to open multidimensional doorways and walk through, not only for ourselves, but for those who come to us for healing and empowerment?

Do you, personally, have this ability and right?

Because, this is what we are doing in Prayers of Intent and Guided Visualizations.

There is a beautiful and delightful (yes, also frightening and maddening) evolution of consciousness going on right now in the times we live in. This last wave started at least 100 years ago and will continue for many, many years. We play our part, perfectly.

People we know, and love, can be caught up in the riptides of any of the previous waves, sure that their perception is the one true reality. We might even be caught up from time to time in a particularly familiar undertow. That is the nature of being in the water (incarnating at this time in history).

Mountain-sized boulders have been thrown into the fabric of our current space and time, and we are in the water as well as on the shore, observing the show. We have multiple perspectives and many times we can feel like we, or loved ones, are drowning in the turbulent waves.

However, as a Lightworker, remember we are also on the rocky shoreline, shining our light, however bright or dimmed it may be. We shine our light of consciousness. We are like electrons, jumping from potential to potential. Orbiting (in probability jumps) our own nucleus. We hold to a higher perspective. We intend our work with pristine clarity and hold no agenda for those beings of love and light who do ask for our help in this time of storm.

Prayers of Intent and Guided Visualizations help us to keep our focus and vision during this time. They help us to open multidimensional doorways in ourselves and in our clients, if they choose. They help us cross veils that were only crossed by Shamans.

Are you a Shaman? Yes, a Lightworker is a Shaman, but one designed to work for these times we live in. Lightly.

Chapter 2

Quantum Connections

Taking our personal cosmologies a step further, let's spend a little time with our inner world, and discern more clearly 'Who' or 'What' is in there.

After reviewing the last chapter, your personal cosmology, if you have determined that your inner world is not populated by any discarnate energy or Being (Spirit), that is perfectly acceptable. Trust your inner discernment and work with the energies of healing, quantum, the most expansive scope of your visioning. Trust in that. And, skip this entire chapter!

If you are not sure what you believe, or Who you might believe in, then I would recommend working through this chapter, opening your mind to the possibilities of various Beings of Love and Light.

Is it wishful thinking to believe in Angels?

Is it fantasy to believe in a Supreme Being?

Did Jesus really live and is He still accessible to us through time and space?

Is any Master who has ever lived available to us now?

These are all very interesting and powerful considerations!

Belief and faith are extremely important. However, spontaneous healing and the effects of placebos work even in the absence of belief and faith. How could healing occur for non-believers? Placebos work through the 'power of expectation' is what we are told by experimental scientists and the research pharmaceutical industry. Belief, expectation, and mind create the strong positive effects, even though the exact procedures are not known or understood.

In the quantum, we are not working with belief, faith, or placebos. We are opening potentialities or doorways into multidimensionality and, with the resonance of our intent and vibrational frequency, calling upon Beings of Love and Light who align in frequency with us and with our clients. It's a mouthful – but it is really simple. It's just physics. It's just about aligning with what is in your range. We do it all the time, when meditate or go into light trance states. It is what we do as energy workers, Lightworkers, in this time of need.

It's physics and resonance. Frequencies that are in range of each other, can attract one another, can 'read' one another.

Plasticizing Time and Space

The first law of thermodynamics, the Law of Conservation, states that energy cannot be created or destroyed. It can only be transferred or changed from one form to another.

Is Personal Consciousness energy?

Is Universal Consciousness behind this cosmic dance?

Can we, through intent, open and step through the quantum, into limitless possibility, to call upon and bring forth Beings of Love and Light through multiple dimensions of time and space, and help set the stage for healings?

These are all interesting points to consider when we are working with our inner populated worlds!

Physicists are stating that time is a dimension, along with space. The three dimensions (length, width, depth) increase to include this 4th dimension, time/space, an accepted worldview for over 100 years. It is human bias, through our filtered and protected mind-scapes, to think we only access the present.

The Mayans, Shamans, and a handful of modern day scientists and visionaries believe time is cyclical, time is accessible – both past and future as well as present. Gregg Braden, in his fascinating book, Fractal Time, describes large cycles of history repeating itself, once the seed event is identified. In the movie, Arrival, time is shown to be circular, and the future impacts the present with mind-boggling precision and mind-bending logic.

Reiki 2 attunes us to symbols that allow us to cross the barrier to the past, to the future, and throughout all space. You can send back to yourself as a child. You can send to yourself 2 years from now. You can send to a loved one across the world. You can send to loved ones who have transitioned. Time and space are not barriers to sending Reiki healing energies.

Experience this for yourself!

Send back and forth through time and space and keep documentation of what occurs. In my experience, there are waves of Reiki waiting for me when I send to the future. And, when I send to the past, it takes a little time for it to 'bubble up' to the present. But, change occurs. Just as our physicists predict!

So, if energy cannot be destroyed, only transformed, and, if we can reach across the time/space barrier, then…. why not connect with, learn from, dialogue with, and enjoy the company of the Luminaries who shine their light throughout eternity?

Why wouldn't They be there for us?

My Full Circle Journey

As a very young child, I put myself to sleep at night by crossing my feet, imagining nails going in my hands and feet, thorns digging into my head, crying that I (somehow) did such terrible things that Jesus was tortured and died for me. (Did I not listen to my parents enough? Was I unkind to my sisters? What, oh what, could I have done?)

Catholic high school and college was supposed to have cemented my faith, but, instead, it did the opposite. I learned too much of Church history and became furious over the Church's misogynistic stance on women in the priesthood and the (continued) rejection of birth control. As a young woman in her early 20's, this unconscionable position was – and still is! – irrational, abusive, intrusive, deeply wounding to women around the world, and contributes to hunger, homelessness, mental distress, and searing poverty in the most vulnerable populations.

As a psychology and counseling student, it surprised me to learn that experts in the field of psychology discounted any religious experience or mindset, seeing it akin to superstitious nonsense and fantasy, bordering on mental illness. Childlike and ignorant at best. I was taught during the 'behavioral psychology' years, that consciousness and the inner life either doesn't exist at all, or, if they do, it's nothing to do with our field of mental health. We were scientists! We were rational! We only deal in laboratory experiments (torturing animals). I was taught to I needed to forget internal realities, and work to change others' behaviors using a (very small) psychological tool kit.

The next decade, during my doctoral years, the field expanded from 'behavior-only' to include clients' thoughts ('cognitive-behavioral'), which were likened to a computer system. A breakthrough for psychology! The mind was seen as a giant computer, taking in data and spitting out information. Change the input, change the output. Psychological theory has always seemed to me like a nerdy kid playset, changing words and theories whenever the prevailing winds blew, without a true understanding of the Being within Human Being.

In between these two mindsets (behaviorism and cognitive behaviorism), I turned instead to an inner meditative, Eastern oriented philosophy and daily meditative practice. During these decades of my life, I closed my mind to Jesus, Mary, Angels and those Beings who were originally my closest allies and shut out most of what I was taught in my psychology and counseling classes, only bringing forth their theories for exams. Instead, I practiced going within to find out Who and What was really there.

Surprisingly for me, I hated meditating! My mind was too active, and I was deluged from thoughts that swirled me into bottomless depths of family pain. I never felt 'good enough'. I had a longing for devotion – but to Whom and for what? I had thrown out childhood images of heaven. Hell I threw out decades before - how could I be happy when I knew my beloved relatives were rotting in hell for all eternity for not following church rules? Strange 'God'. Strange beliefs. I didn't like to be controlled by fear and male hierarchies.

Four decades later, in the strangest way, I took a Reiki class and found that I had come full circle! The Reiki Master who attuned me, Ellen Louise Kahn, a devout Jewish woman, taught me an ancient system which was channeled in from a Japanese man who was probably working within a Buddhist framework.

And, paradoxically, she spoke to me about working, through Reiki, with Jesus, Mary, and the Angels. At first it was like opening a creaky, stuck door. Jesus, again? Mary?

t has been quite a journey for me. I resisted at first, but Ellen's stories of working with Jesus and Mary were compelling and I found myself, slowly, hesitatingly, opening myself to those Realities once again. And, it has been mind and heart opening!

Honoring Our Client's Journey

With a new client, before we start the session, I ask them what their 'personal cosmology' is. Do they pray to anyone in particular?

Common answers include "Jesus", "Angels", or "I'm not really sure – the Universe I guess". This discussion can begin to allow an opening to occur within the client before any work is done on the table. They are acknowledging the Beings of Love and Light who they wish to connect with, or, they are acknowledging that there is a possibility that there is more in their lives to be experienced.

I consciously use the words, 'personal cosmology', rather than ask about their religion or their spirituality. This is a gentle way of circumventing prior conditionings. It offers the client a way to reframe their beliefs and experiences, their hopes and fears, their anticipations for Invited Guests and Beloveds to visit during the session.

Often a client asks if I can contact a family member who has departed or a special Light Being (such as their Guardian Angel or Jesus).

My response is the same – sometimes I get information for them from Someone we call in. I can't promise to do this, as I always ask for the 'Highest and Greatest Good for All'. With that condition in mind, we sometimes do get information and visits, and sometimes we don't.

This serves two purposes: it sets the expectations appropriately for the client and removes any pressure on me to perform. Best if we don't have an agenda other than 'Highest and Greatest Good for All'. We are included in the 'All'. The client is included in the 'All'. Everyone in their circle, incarnated or not, is included in the 'All'.

However, for those times the person they ask for is not present, I begin to silently ask (beg) for a symbol or a message of some kind for the client and their specific intent. I am both adamant and humbling, but I do not want to say to a client, "Sorry, I've got nothing for you. No one came." How would that serve them?

The concentrated effort of asking, adamant and humbling, never fails to work for me. I will get a symbol, an understanding of what is going on for them within higher patterns, a chakra to be looked at again, a color, an etheric gift, an angelic name – it varies for each client. In an infinite universe, help always comes.

Finally, I ask a new client if it's OK with them if I say a Prayer of Intent. Almost always they respond, "Yes!

I check in with them about their intent, how I might expand upon it for them, and let them know Who I am calling in for them. Again, our intent is to allow the client the security, safety, and resonance of highest frequency so that they may ascend into their healing space during the session.

We set the structure, open the portals, sing, invite, visualize, intend, create and hold the space. The client and their Guides, on their personal soul contracted destiny path, are the ones who affect the healing and empowering changes.

Placebos show belief and expectation can work miracles. In the Quantum Consciousness we are not intending or asking to work miracles. We are setting expectations, working with probabilities, and pulling upon the fabric of 'reality' as the true conscious creators, at the leading edge of thought that we and our clients are!

'We' are not the ones 'doing' the healing for another. Although many have thanked me for their healings, I do not take credit and, similarly, I do not take blame. I understand that we are each Divine Creators and, with our Soul Contracts, we choose this destiny path, albeit on a soul level, not a personality level. I call upon the Beings of Love and Light whom I choose to, and am Guided to, work with, and I am also sensitive to those Beings of Love and Light who align with clients.

Who are these Beings?

Inviting Quantum Connections
Through Time and Space

The Beings of Love and Light are beyond time and space. They may have walked the earth thousands of years ago, but they are able to appear and respond to your call immediately. Time doesn't exist in the quantum. They may have lived halfway around the world. Space doesn't exist in the quantum.

There are interesting experiments which are called 'quantum entanglement'. Connected particles respond immediately, faster than the speed of light, even if they are separated across the universe. The 'field' encompasses All There Is.

Make the call.

Invite with intent.

Allow for the Invited to appear.

Dialogue.

If I can do this work, so can you!

We all have the ability. It is built in.

There is nothing to feel worthy or unworthy about.

Unworthiness is an old belief structure (see Chapter 1). To call in the Divine, and to work with Them in your healing practice is the most sublime and humbling experience! It does not mean you are on a pedestal. You are in service to the Divine. What could be more humbling than that?

Book 4 of the Tools for Lightworkers Series, Dialogue with Spirit, details many of these magnificent Beings of Love and Light that you can call upon in your Prayer of Intent and your Guided Visualizations.

These include:

> Source, Creator, God, the Divine Constellation
>
> Your Soul, Your Higher Self, Your Guardian Angel
>
> Angels and Archangels
>
> Jesus, Mary, and Magdalen, Tower of Strength
>
> Ascended Masters
>
> Buddha, Quan Yin, Bodhisattvas through the ages
>
> Spiritual Luminaries
>
> Holy Ones, Sages and Saints
>
> Overlighting Earth Angels
>
> Archetypal Energies
>
> Multidimensional Beings of Love and Light
>
> Councils of Light and Lightworker Grids
>
> > ARISE Lightworker Grid
> >
> > Reiki Lightworker Grid
> >
> > Gaia Lightworker Grid
> >
> > Global Lightworker Grid
> >
> > Galactic Lightworker Grid
> >
> > Council of Light
> >
> > Consortium of Peacemakers

Rather than repeat the information provided in Dialogue with Spirit about these Beings of Love and Light, I share some personal Visits with you, below.

Jesus and Friends

The first time I 'saw' **Jesus**, He seemed to come from the wall in front of me, as if He were stepping out of a stained-glass window. He stepped forward, put His hands on the client and silently worked on her. I was amazed and humbled.

Jesus is known for hands-on healing and His work within the Reiki system is well known. Once, with a client, Cara, on the Reiki table, I heard the name, "Joseph" and said, "Someone named Joseph is here for you."

Next, I heard, "Ben." Ben Joseph? Who could that be? Finally, I heard, "Jeshua".

Oh! Jeshua ben Joseph! Jesus announcing himself in Hebrew? It's always fun and astounding working in the inner realms.

*

Jesus and Mary both appeared to me in the early morning hours of my gall bladder attack, one on each side of me. Jesus put His hands directly inside my body and the pain, miraculously, stopped. When he took His hands out and the pain returned, I knew it was time to go to urgent care.

*

Mother Mary comes as a beautiful, loving Presence, many times surrounded with blue light. The first time I 'saw' Mary she approached the table of a client, Kay, who was going to have a double mastectomy the following day. Mary approached the table with white linens over her arm. The 'message' that I intuited was that Mary was going to be with her in the hospital, during recovery. Not to worry. And, her surgery went well.

*

A client, Jill, fostered over 50 children and the toll it had taken upon her body was great. As I was doing Reiki for her, I 'saw' water falling onto barren ground and beautiful white flowers growing from the water. I then realized it was not rain, but tears falling from the sky. Wondering Who was crying, I looked up and 'saw' Quan Yin. Her face was as large as a moon and I saw her profile. I had never worked with Quan Yin before and was amazed. As I recounted this to Jill, she seemed unfazed. "Oh, I pray to Quan Yin all the time! I'm not surprised she showed up." I was!

*

The **Holy Spirit** came for a session for a client, Stephanie. I had never worked with this Deity and was amazed at the creative and loving sphere of energy that comes. Again, like Jill, Stephanie was nonchalant about the Visit and remarked afterwards that she prays devotedly to the Holy Spirit daily and has for many years.

*

The same experience occurred with Asha and **Guru Nanak**. I had not worked with him before but felt a Presence in the middle of Asha's session. I did not know his name or recognize him, although I knew he was a Guru. I asked, and received 'Nanak', and hesitantly mentioned the name to Asha. She laughingly told me she had been singing bhajans, which are Hindu devotional songs to Guru Nanak just before she came for a session. She was devoted to him. Nanak appeared very loving, humorous, and connected to Asha.

*

Shirley was an older woman and I knew she was a lifelong devotee of **Gurdjieff**, a mystic and spiritual teacher from the early 1900's. I had heard of him but was not drawn to his followers or their philosophies. Shirley was dying and wanted a session. Although I had preconceived notions about Gurdjieff, I was humbled and amazed when I 'saw' him appear for Shirley, kiss her on her forehead, and then give her a hand to help her transition up and out of her body. So much for my judgments!

*

Archangels come often for a session and I call upon them in my Prayers of Intent often. **Archangel Michael** is a favorite for many. He is a Shield and a Protector and is very aligned with energy healing.

Archangel Raphael is known as a healing angel. Feel free to call upon him anytime. Once, with a counseling student, Lorna, who was working on deep emotional woundings, I heard the name, 'Ray El'. I asked and was told this was a Being to call on for mental and emotional healings. This Being also works specifically with counselors and therapists. I was excited to tell her about this special Guide and it was weeks before I realized that 'Ray El' was actually 'Raphael'. Angels do love to play with us!

Archangel Chamuel is a wonderful angel to call upon for relationships. Metatron for spiritual teachings. Uriel for transitions of all kinds. There are so many wonderful angel books, audios, and card decks. If you are drawn to work with angels, it helps to know some of their names and their specialties.

*

 'Those Who Hold the Vibrational Records' is the way I phrase accessing past life information for a client.

*

 'Those Who Work with DNA Activation' and **'Rejuvenation and Restoration'** are other Guide Groups who work with us in advanced healing sessions. These most frequently are found within the Crystal Chambers and the Hall of Healing Masters, found in Guided Visualizations, part 4.

*

Loved Ones Who Have Transitioned is the way I call upon those family and loved ones of a client who they ask to call to the healing table. In the past, this was known as 'mediumship' and I never thought I could do this, or even wanted to do this. It seemed spooky and scary, just like in the movies.

However, when a client would mourn and grieve about a Loved One, I started inviting them in.

I can't say they come all the time, but, many times they do! With Melanie, it was an upcoming holiday and her children were with their father. She recounted sweet memories of cooking with her mother for the traditional holiday feast. I asked her Mom to come in and be with her and I 'saw' her mom in a white apron. I asked Melanie if she had one, or if her Mom always wore a special one. No, on both counts. Although, not so large a leap from cooking to apron, so I gave it no more thought, except to tell Melanie that perhaps she might want to buy one for herself, to remember her Mom as she was alone on this special day.

Less than a week later I got a surprising text message with a picture of Melanie in a Wonder Woman apron, complete with the superhero costume against a white background. Her youngest daughter felt inspired to buy it for Melanie before she left for her dad's house. She had never gotten a gift for her mom before, and Melanie never mentioned our session, or the apron, to anyone.

Coincidence? Miracle? Normal for Quantum Entanglement?

*

Once I attended a teleconference on mediumship from a psychology department in the University of Phoenix. They designed a '5 blind study' of people who lost Loved Ones and those who said they could communicate with people who have passed (mourners and mediums). The results were beyond the 99% range of statistical significance.

During the following question and answer period, I mentioned (hesitantly) that I was an energy healer and was able to sometimes do this work – but how? I never could do it before. The conference leader answered that people are starting to come forward, (in his academic setting, a college psychology lab) saying this communication style comes to them with enough practice, if they are open to the possibility that it can happen. The professor said, in his opinion, if we knew, beyond any doubt, that our Loved Ones still exist, and that we could dialogue with them, "everything would change" in the world. Interesting to ponder! Who would you want to contact? What would you want to say? What if it were real?

*

Mark came for his Mother, Janet, showing up with a red rose and a love poem for her. Janet still grieved for her 'bad boy' who was a rowdy college student, who, for years, had been drinking and doing drugs. Mark was alienated from his family before he died aspirating after a night of binging. His death occurred almost 10 years before I met Janet. Mark immediately came in for his Mom's healing session with a poem in hand, some lines of which I could read. How could I possibly know that Mark used to write poems to his Mom when he was a young boy, and that she had his poems framed on her wall?

*

Evan, a beautiful young boy who transitioned at 1 ½ years old from a drowning, came for his Dad when I asked Joseph to pull an oracle card for a job change he was going through. He had gotten that particular job when Evan transitioned 10 years before and he was now just losing that customer. It brought up a lot of old feelings of grief and remorse. The card Joseph picked was from an Inner Child card deck. The Little Prince, by Antoine de Saint- Exupery, said, 'a young boy came to Earth for a very short time to teach a special man the power of love'. You can believe I cried for that session.

*

Archetypal Energies, especially the **Inner Child**, are wonderful to call in for a healing session.

Over 30 years ago, I met my Inner Child during a light trance state I entered on my 1½ hour subway commute from Queens to Manhattan. She was about 5 years old and lived in our old apartment house. She and I went through a closet door in my old bedroom and, Narnia-style, we emerged in another time and place. Wooded, serene and soothing, we came upon a log cabin and fixed it up just like we wanted to, with furniture, food, books and art supplies. The setting was unforgettable.

I was shocked when it was time to come home - she refused to come! I begged and pleaded, not wanting to leave her all alone (what would happen to me without my Inner Child by my side?), but she insisted she would be fine and come visit when I could. I visited again once or twice but forgot after a while.

Years went by and we moved from NY to Oregon, initially to a rural area. The scene out our window looked familiar somehow and, at first, I couldn't remember why it reminded me of something. I had never been in such a rural area before. Then, the entire memory of that fateful subway ride descended upon me like a full packet. I was shocked!

I couldn't bring that sweet Inner Child back to our old NYC apartment. But, she managed to bring me to her, to this serene and soothing area. She brought me across the entire country, to my home, and to her.

When we work in the quantum, things are not what they seem!

*

Qualities

As with archetypes, Qualities can be named and called in for your Prayer of Intent.

Mercy

Forgiveness

Empowerment

Clarity

Stepping into Mastery

Abundance

Connection with the Divine

Increase of Intuitive Gifts

The Beloved

Peace

Allowing

These Qualities and more I have called upon with clients. They have a signature vibration as do energy glyphs and sacred symbols taught in Reiki, Language of Light and Fractal EnLilghtenment classes which we teach at Arise. See Tools for Lightworkers Series books, 8, 9 and 10 for more on these energy glyphs/light languages.

'Seeing' and 'Hearing' Light Beings

I was not a person who ever thought I could see or hear from Beings of Love and Light. The more I practiced Reiki and healing arts, the more my skills began to develop. They start slowly but, once barriers within us (probably our beliefs and sense of unworthiness - two of the strongest barriers) begin to thin, the magic begins!

There are scientists brave enough to experiment in the 'extra sense' or psi arena, such as Rupert Sheldrake, Lothar Schafer, Dean Radin, and others from the Noetic Sciences Institute. Through their work we find there is more than enough evidence compiled. Extra senses are not really extra. They are built in all of us, like our 3D version of sight, hearing, touching, smelling and tasting.

Clairvoyance (clear seeing), clairaudience (clear hearing), clairsentience (clear feeling), claircognizance (clear knowing) and others are higher on the frequency scale than we are taught, from infancy, that we can access. But, we can raise up to them. Practice and releasing fear and self-judgment helps!

Follow the path of your own unique journey. Go within and come to terms with your inner world. Open the doors! Play within this paradigm. Follow the whispers and allow yourself to be courted by the Divine.

For me it has been a wonderful journey within and I no longer have to lay awake at night with the thought of nails pounding into me. Let's all move this energy forward!

Quantum entanglement is real and works effortlessly on our behalf and for the benevolence of our clients. We are connected, faster than light speed, to Beings of Love and Light. Bodhisattvas are those who refuse to leave this earth realm until all are enlightened. We truly have Friends in High Places!

These timeless Energies align on Light Grids around our planet, working for the Light Quotient to tip more towards light than darkness. It might seem, right now, that we are in the midst of dark storms, but, consider when you clean a closet, basement or attic. The amount of dust, useless items, and mess is enough to wonder why we started in the first place. Light shines on all the hidden and dusty areas. So, too, at this time of shift! Transparency is on the rise, as is global awareness that We Are All One.

Take a journey into your Inner Landscape. Who are you inviting in for the Prayer of Intent? Who is joining you in your Guided Visualization?

God and the Divine Constellation

What images does the name 'God' bring up for you? For many, the naming comes with authoritarian beliefs and hierarchical systems. Interestingly, many clients say they are not sure if there is a God or not, but they do believe in Angels! A sure sign of competing paradigms in play.

What does God mean for you?

If you do believe in God – what are God's attributes?

What are some names you feel comfortable calling upon for the highest order (putting 'God' aside for a moment): Divine Mind, Source, Creator, Essence, All There Is, etc.?

It's good to consider possibilities of God names and attributes, so you are more of an expansive and intuitive advocate for your clients, rather than imposing your worldview and nomenclature on them. Brainstorm how you would call upon the Unnamable and Ineffable.

The Goddess in All Her Guises

About 30 years ago, the Goddess began to show up again. She has been 're-membered', in that she has been dug up from the ground in iconic forms and has also been dug up from our ancient memories. So wonderful to have Her back!

There are many ways to call upon the Mothering Presence, the Feminine Energies, the Maiden/ Mother/ Matriarch/ and Crone. Not happy with your weight or body type? Find some pictures of the Venus of Willendorf and call upon the Fulsome Goddess. The Goddess has been revered in ancient times throughout the world civilizations until the patriarchal millennia that we are currently leaving. Matriarchal rites and devotions were prevalent in ancient, communal, and nature- based societies.

As we spiral forward, the blending of the Divine Masculine and the Divine Feminine brings us all into wholeness. Morama/ Morata/ Moreah are advanced light language glyphs in our Fractal EnLightenment, Book 9 Tools for Lightworkers Series. Morama is Divine Feminine. Morata is the Divine Masculine. Moreah is Unified Consciousness.

For those clients who would relax and surrender their healing and empowerment to the Goddess energies, invest time to become familiar with this Emerging and All-Pervasive Presence.

Are there ways you would like to call upon the Mothering Presence?

Angels and Archangels

Do you believe in incarnated energies as Angels and Archangels?

Where did you get this belief?

Do you have actual experiences of Angels?

If so, how do they manifest for you?

Would you like to work with these celestial energies of love, light, mission and purpose? Calling upon the Angels and Archangels can be the beginning of a wonderful partnership and dialogue. Angels have specific missions and purposes. There are Angels and Archangels who are well known within the healing and lightwork communities and work with people all over the globe.

*

Archangel Michael is one of the most called upon Archangels. His name means, 'Who is like God'. He is associated with strength, safety, and security. He works in clearing fear, anxiety, and lower energies. Calling upon Michael and drawing the Reiki symbol, Cho Ku Rei is a wonderful protection for yourself and for conducting a healing session.

*

Archangel Raphael is associated with healing energies, as his name suggests, 'God heals'. When working with Raphael you will receive messages, dreams, and intuitive insights into the situation and ways to subtly alter the dis-ease. He is called upon for Reiki healing sessions and also to help those who wish to introduce alternative methods for health and wellness.

*

Archangel Gabriel is the messenger Angel in the Bible announcing Mary's pregnancy. Gabriel's name translates to 'God is my strength'. Visioned at times as a male and at other times as a female Angel, Gabriel brings messages with intuitive and loving parenting advice about pregnancy, childbirth, raising children, and even connecting with our own Inner Child. She works with writings and communications of all kind.

*

Archangel Uriel's name means, 'God is my light'. Uriel can light your way forward, especially in dark or lost situations, and at transitions, including hard diagnoses. Uriel shines the light of God on choices, life paths, and discerning and following your mission and purpose.

*

Archangel Chamuel is associated with relationships and soul mates. His name means, 'He who sees God', and in relationships it is divine to see the Beloved in your beloved. Chamuel works with peace – internally, in relationships, between countries, and even interspecies. He also works with seeing clearly and bringing clarity to our goals and dreams, especially career related.

*

Archangel Metatron, is associated with spiritual knowledge and sacred geometry. Literally interpreted as 'Beyond the matrix', Metatron is associated with scribing, spiritual knowledge and sacred geometry, especially Metatron's Cube, a 13 sphered Merkabah or light body geometry grid. Metatron also is called upon to work with sensitive and intuitive children. Have you or would you like to work with Metatron?

Are there other Angels or Archangels you work with?

Your Guardian Angel is said to be with you for this lifetime (and others if your model of reality allows for this occurrence). *Have you had an experience of your Guardian Angel? Would you like to? Have you had a desperate experience or crisis and felt the gentle embrace or saving touch of this personal Guard?*

Oriel is my personal Angelic Guide and you can read her words through my writing in Book 4 of the *Tools for Lightworkers Series, Dialogue with Spirit.*

She gives instructions for automatic writing and conversations with Oriel are included in that book.

Jesus

Jesus, also known as Jeshua ben Joseph, preached and lived words of love, equality, social justice, compassion, forgiveness, and peace, both inner and outer.

In Reiki, Jesus is welcomed and often comes to the healing session. Some religious or institutionalized groups may believe they are the only ones who access the Christed, or Unconditional Love Energies. This might be your path, or it might be the path you abandoned. Nevertheless, working your way through these thousands-of- years-tangled-threads is worthwhile if you wish to feel comfortable calling upon Jesus, The Christed Energies, Unconditional Love and Light.

(Please note that many clients only align with Jesus for their healing. Reflect and consider calling upon only Jesus to be present for them.)

Mary

Mary is hidden in plain sight. There have been many global, apparitions of Mary, bringing messages of love and peace. As the Divine Mother energies for western worlds, Mary is available for healing sessions and brings her blue cloak, her blue light, to wrap around us and around clients in times of desperation and need. Call upon her for nurturing and dedicated love through all travails.

Saints, Sages and the Tower of Strength

Mary Magdalene has been confounded and conflated with a generic 'Mary' in the Bible as the prostitute who had demons released and who washed Jesus' feet with her hair. Nowhere in the Bible was it said that person was Mary Magdalene! More recent information, especially garnered through the lost scrolls, shows that Mary Magdalene was an important disciple of Jesus's and that she shared in his ministry. In Aramaic, 'magdala' means tower.

50

Mary was the Tower of Strength and has been linked as Jesus's wife and partner, although this relationship is lost in the veils of time.

Mary Magdalene appeared in a healing session I was offering for a young man, Bob, who was falsely accused of a sexual attack. He was dealing with the legal and personal aftermath of being wrongfully accused. Mary, the Tower of Strength, came and embraced his Inner Child, rocking and soothing him, serving as his anchor for a moment out of time, in this particularly ferocious storm. The Tower of Strength is all embracing and works well with those who feel injustice has been done.

Buddhist and Hindu Deities: Quan Yin, Buddha, Avalokitesvara, Green Tara and White Tara

These Beings work on the highest octaves of love and light and are often invoked by healers and Lightworkers.

The Buddha has been revered by millions of people for thousands of years. He is known, affectionately, as the Buddha of Joy and the Buddha of Enlightenment. His qualities are many including patience, wisdom, loving kindness, deep reflection, truthfulness, highest ethics and integrity. We dearly need these qualities in our times today!

Quan Yin/ Kuan Yin is a well- known and beloved Buddhist deity whose name translates to "She Who Hears the Prayers of the World". She is often associated as the equivalent female deity to Mary, although each Beloved Woman has a unique signature frequency; they can be enjoyed in unison or uniquely. Quan Yin is known as a Boddhisatva – one who has chosen to stay and work on behalf of humanity until all are enlightened. Known as Kannon in Japan, she is also associated with Tibetan Tara.

Avalokitesvara is a Buddhist diety, pictured as the male form of Quan Yin. He is known to work compassionately on the behalf of all humanity – thus, he is also known as a Boddhisatva. In Karuna Reiki Master, the Sanskrit name of Avalokitesvara is translated as "the Sound that Illumines the World", thus an appropriate and inspiring energy to call upon for sound healing.

Lakshmi is the Hindu deity of abundance, health, beauty and prosperity.

Ganesh is the Hindu deity who removes all obstacles.

> *Are there special Masters and Teachers, Poets and Sages you wish to call upon?*

Benevolent Energies

Along with those Beings mentioned above, there are times and sessions you wish to call upon other, less well- known energies. Here are some to consider:

Reiki Guides and Energies are always appropriate to call upon when conducting a Reiki session, for your Prayer of Intent. There are many wonderful higher Beings associated with Reiki including Jesus, Mary, Buddha, and Quan Yin. You may feel drawn to invite in the people we know who have been instrumental in bringing Reiki to the world. This includes Mikao Usui, the one who channeled Reiki back into the world, Churiyo Hiyashi, and Hawayo Takata, the woman who brought Reiki to the west.

Gaia is our Earth Mother. It is wonderful to partner and dialogue with Gaia. The Planetary Consciousness is an extremely high frequency awareness and, as we are an intimate partner, we are able to work directly with Gaia. Call upon the Earth Mother energies for grounding, for work with the weather, natural disasters, and all types of global, communal, interspecies and personal issues. For example, if you want to discern a wonderful location for you to move, call upon Gaia. If you want to work directly with drought conditions, refugee resettlements, food and water for all, or specific animal changes, call upon Gaia to work with you.

For animal companions, call upon the Overlighting Animal Energies. For example, you can call upon, Feline Angels, Canine Angels, or Equine Angels for your beloved companions. Although animals incarnate as part of a particular group consciousness, those who are named and loved by you personally have access to a larger Guide set, outside their group consciousness. They can work with you as your Animal Guide! You can call upon loved companions who have transitioned to be with you.

In our SoulAngel Harmonics, those of the 'Dinal' lineage feel called to work with animals as a strong service in this life. You can read more of this in Book 11, SoulAnge Harmonics, in the Tools for Lightworkers Series. You can also send healing energies for special groups such as Angels for Lost, Stray, and Feral Companion Animals, Angels for Lab Purpose Animals, and Angels for Food Consumption Animals.

Conscious Energies and Qualities can be called upon in the Prayer of Intent and Guided Visualizations. We can also connect with and call upon superconscious energies and qualities, such as the Solar Angel, the Heart of the Mother (galactic center or 'black hole'), and Multidimensional Beings of Love and Light (galactic and stellar travelers).

The Sacred Heart energies, which I call the Serami Amor, Serami Ador, heart flame, in Fractal EnLightenment, is wonderful for those who have their hearts broken open and are in need of deep heart healing.

Eternal Connections

As you can see, there are so many wonderful Beings, Energies, Qualities, and Luminaries that you can call upon in your Prayer of Intent and to visit in your Guided Visualizations. Practice, an open mind and an open heart will take you far! These Beings are eternal. We are connected to them through all time, space and dimension. They await our call. They respond always. "Knock and it is given unto you."

> Which Ones would you like to call upon for yourself and your connection?

> Which Ones would you like to call upon for your client's intent? Who do they want?

Some guidelines are considered in Part 2, Orchestral Prelude, that will help you refine your work, increase your intuitive gifts, and allow you to believe more in yourself, your abilities, and your Highest Destiny path of service!

Part 2

Orchestral

Prelude

Introduction

In Part 2, Orchestral Prelude, we cover two important preparations for opening quantum doorways.

The third chapter, Suite Overture, has information which sets the stage for both Prayers of Intent and Guided Visualizations. These are basic understandings and skills, and I recommend that you check out this 3rd chapter before jumping in to the parts you are drawn to in this book.

Chapter 4, Vocal Harmonics, list titles of songs and chants offered for beginning, middle and ending of energy healing sessions. Beginning harmonics are detailed in Chapter 4. Middle session harmonics are included in detail in Part 3, Prayer of Intent. End session harmonics are included in detail in Part 4, Guided Visualizations.

Chapter 3

Suite Overture

A few years ago, my neighbor offered me a ticket to attend a classical performance at our gilded, traditional venue, the Arlene Schnitzer Concert Hall. I hadn't been to a classical performance before and thought it would be fun to try something new. Although I loved to hear my daughter practice her classical piano pieces at home, my music nourishment came almost exclusively from CD's, my phone, and laptop – not live instruments.

I wasn't prepared for the sound experience of a stage of vibrating harmonies. I was enraptured as the energies moved through the hall and found me all the way up in the 1st balcony. It was mesmerizing to see the players as well. The percussionist might prepare the entire piece, standing at attention, slowly moving back the velvet piece of cloth, mallet in hand, for one light sounding 'gong'. Not even a finale crashing moment, just one subtle undertone.

I was hooked! We got season tickets and every month I felt and learned something new. It was also a wonderful inspirational birthing ground for many SoulAnge Harmonic lineages which I sing in for clients, and for many Fractal EnLightenment energy glyphs. I get my inspirations normally during light trance states and in the shower. Silence and water are wonderful conductors and open doorways within. Music is also a well- known conductor and opener. Live music, with dozens of consummate musicians, perfectly attuned to their instruments, playing soaring, inspired vocabularies was sublime. I realized the similarities to our work.

The magnificent harmonics of a specially designed orchestra interweave its varying instrument families. The four basic types are distinguished based upon the way they produce vibrations. And, as in Our Orchestra, vibrations are the keyThe strings pluck and pierce our everyday soundscapes, bringing both melody and harmony. The percussions usher in vibrant, rhythmic, trance inducing states; they are in the right place at the right time with the right strike force. Breath is the key for both brass and woodwinds. One, brash, directional, using lip tension and air flow. The other, quieter, non-directional, melodic and heart soaring. Then, we have the conductor, the music score, and the audience.

Consider Prayers of Intent and Guided Visualizations as our Orchestral gift to ourselves and our clients. We bring in all the tools at our level of expertise. We can breathe. Use breath. We can speak. Use vocal tones. We can call upon the Beings of Love and Light to sing with us and through us. We have our musical score in front of us and we are our own Conductors – dancing this dream awake.

Practice Beforehand

Get to know your instruments. You are going to play all of them! Listen and decide upon the types of musical sound that inspires you and play that in the background. Use the sounds as a base to move from. Do you like the rhythm? Hum and sway to the beat. Do you like the words? Use them in your Prayers and Visualizations, and then allow your own words to come forth. Capture your inspirations on your phone recorders or on paper.

The more you feel comfortable using your voice as your instrument, the more rewards and presents.

Use Your Own Words and Metaphors

Honor your vocabulary, your cadence, and your inner poetry.

Each of us has our Inner Mystic, Inner Poet, Inner Celebrant so allow your images and vocabulary to bubble up from within. The sample Prayers and Visualizations I offer are meant to encourage and inspire you. For any that feel good to you, align with your heart center, or inspire you to expand – feel free to use. Experiment and allow your words to come forth.

The sacred spaces I offer in Guided Visualizations are many which I have walked or dreamt. Use these as jumping off points for your own personal, unique, sacred experiences and expressions. Feel free to innovate and to liven up both the prayers and the visualizations with sacred and inspired spaces you have walked and dreamed.

Repetition and Ritual

Just as a river stays alive by flowing this way and that, learn to trust your inner voice and your inner muse to follow your intent. This will keep your Prayers and Visualizations living, organic, and divinely inspired.

Ritual is a well- known and well-traversed pathway that can soothe our minds and allow us to slip into sacred space through the repetition. Consider the comfort if you have ever prayed a rosary or if you have repeated a phrase or mantra, especially a sacred one. There is a sense of timelessness and serenity imbued within the practice.

Your Prayers of Intent and Guided Visualizations might fall into this abiding, sacred category so that you welcome the intonations as a special friend, one who takes your hand and leads you through the portal into divine space for healing, balance and empowerment.

Be aware, though, that ritual can also become a habit where we go into autopilot mode and repeat the words for the sake of repeating them. Here, the power has been lost. The delicious pathways of the ever-running river can start to become muddied and dammed. If this happens, jazz it up by changing one or two parts, or, consider creating a completely new composition.

I often play with words and images until one Prayer of Intent and one Guided Visualization is polished to a gem state. This, then, leads me to the quickly ascending escalator which brings me to a multidimensional state in a very short amount of time. Sometimes, within the space of a breath or two.

After years, I seem to forget the arrangement, or it fails to deliver. I then play, hum, sing, do symbols, until the next sequence arrives. It's up to you to discern the path and to follow it accordingly.

Design Your 'Musical Score'

It helps to have a Prayer of Intent and Guided Visualization in mind before your session or training class. You can always enhance or subtract from it, depending upon your intuition at the time, and your client's comfort levels.

Having a written, step-by-step 'score' next to you can help immeasurably. You can relax and be at ease, knowing that you won't forget anything you deem important. You can be more in the moment and feel your way through each part of the process.

However, I recommend *not reading* your Prayer of Intent or your Guided Visualization! Know enough of your presentation so that words or outlines can prompt you. You can underline or highlight important areas. You can put Reiki symbols to help you access your higher wisdom and trust that what you say is in the 'highest and greatest good for all' (especially if you include that phrase in your Prayer).

Reading a script takes the immediacy and 'quantumness' from your work. You are not fully present – you are acting a part. You need to be living your part, vibrating your part. In an orchestra, the flute players don't say – 'flute solo' – they play it. They vibrate it. You need to vibrate it. And you can do this more easily when you are feeling, not reading.

Fine Tune Your Instruments

Your Instruments of Breath

Like our wood winds and brass instruments, use your breath!

Start with a short breath journey – bringing their attention down their body with each breath and then into the earth is an easy one. This signals the beginning of relaxing and deepening for both you and your client. You also ride upon the breath with these simple words and step between portals. It is a great tool to go within!

Consciously use your breath when you are speaking or intoning your Prayer of Intent and with your Guided Visualizations. Take deep breaths, blow your breath, play with the sounds and feelings until they become an easy part of your repertoire.

Blow the breath over your client's body to help release energies. Breath can free up stuck areas, can smooth over bobbling areas, and can deepen the integration of healing glyphs and symbols.

I use my breath to warm and wake up the palms of my hands before a session. I also blow into my palms my master and healing symbols and glyphs. Sometimes I blow a breath from my client's head down the length of their body. Other times I stand on their side and blow a breath from left and right and envision a blanket of air settling on them. I will also blow from their feet into the earth to help ground.

End with a short breath journey to bring the client (and you) back to everyday reality. Ground with breath into the earth. Gaia is our partner and she helps us release excess or toxic energies, like a shock absorber. You and your client can feel dizzy or woozy by working in the etheric for a while, so breath and Gaia help ground.

Your Instruments of Percussion

Like our orchestral percussion instruments, use a striking resonance to open or close a session. This can be done with a crystal bowl, tuning fork, bell, windchime, drum or other percussion tool.

A light tinkling sound reverberates so softly and sweetly. A deeply resonating tuning sound reaches deep within both of your bodies. Experiment with any of these tools either by striking them yourself or by playing a song with these sounds in the room during your sessions.

Percussion instruments have a long, revered history with indigenous tribes throughout the entire world and throughout our entire human history. Entire communities would obtain inspiration, connection and release through the use of their hands, feet, and simple tools, beating out a message much like our beating heart. Shamans would lead themselves and others through quantum doorways into multidimensionality with a simple bone.

Follow the beat!

Your Instruments of Melodic Strings

Which songs – melodies and lyrics – call to you? Play those for yourself and for your clients. Play them lightly in the background to inspire you. Put the volume up a little higher if you wish to incorporate more of what they are vibrating, both musically and verbally. The array of musical offerings we have available to us at the click of a button is truly astounding. Find your favorites.

The resonance of the strings, themselves, change our frequencies. They help us deepen, they help us soar. They fire our imagination and our devotion. They inspire us and bring us to tears. They open a portal to allow Loved Ones to cross over. They bring us back to our childhoods, our youth, our first loves, our last loves. A song, even a lyric, can change your life.

At the end of this chapter are songs designed for inner work, written by both myself and by Tony, my husband and partner in Arise. See Vocal Harmonics, below for lyrics that might inspire you.

Modulate Your Voice

A word about modulating your voice. When transitioning from normal conversation to a Guided Visualization our voices usually shift from our common vocal patterns to a softer, gentler tone of voice. You are stepping yourself and your client through a portal into a safe, sacred space for healing and a place where higher communications can occur for both of you.

There is a sweet spot between the one-note voice register where everything you say is almost hypnotically spoken and our normal inflections of high's and low's. When people think of giving a Guided Visualization they most times choose this monotone, less reflective, disembodied voice. And that type of patterning may help people relax and even go to sleep.

I encourage you not to stop at lulling someone (yourself and your client) into a light trance state (sleep state). Instead, open quantum doorways! Visualize the portal you are opening and walking through. Visualize the Guests - both invited and surprise visitors. Walk and describe the journey as you go.

Use your conscious intent to open the space up. Speak with a cadence that is soothing, and yet is story-telling, or portal-crossing. Try the variations for yourself. Find a comfortable way of helping yourself and your client shift from 3D to multi-D. Ask for feedback or tape yourself and listen with compassion and clarity to your own voice.

This opening and crossing of portals is done by a confluence of …. your intent, your belief in your words, visualizing your words, and … Grace. In multidimensionality, there is playful probability, not clockwork mechanism. And, in Lightwork, there are Blessings from above. 'Ask and it shall be opened unto you.'

Another recommendation is to allow yourself moving space. I walk and talk the visualization, moving my hands and body to the respective parts on the client. For example, if I speak about roots coming out of the soles of their feet, I move to the foot of the table, and in the air above their feet I motion the 'roots' coming out of their soles and going down to the earth. When I describe the Archway of Flowers, I draw the arch over my head. I breathe in a little stronger and louder to smell the delicious scent.

Allow yourself the freedom to bring your body as well as your voice along with you on the journey.

Silent vs. Vocal

It's a blessing for you and for your clients when you use your voice in a session. This is especially so when saying a Prayer of Intent or Guided Visualization.

However, some days you may not feel like it. Or, you may feel uncomfortable in front of a new client – you may be picking up on their unease or your own self-judgment.

Did you have much experience with musical education in school? You would be lucky if you did! Music, art, using our body kinesthetically – all these critical human expressions are considered 'not relevant' to our present education system. We drain our children like husks, down to a dry academic diet. This quashing of the human spirit, of creativity itself, must and will change as we move forward into the shifting energies. Creativity is as important as food! It is our food. It is life itself.

Luckily, vibrations vibrate, and silent Prayers of Intent are perfectly fine. Be easy with yourself as you begin to claim your voice. Hum. It helps. Silent Guided Visualizations will still help you set the tone of the session - and this, then, will help the client deepen through a resonance with your vibration. It's just a subtler experience. Free yourself from criticism. Take it step by step. There is a reason we have been robbed of our inner harmony and our voices.

As you might expect, it does quicken and enhance the experience for both yourself and your client so much more when it is vocal. How to get from hesitation, embarrassment, lack of experience, shame, fear of using our voice to a confident, courageous Lightworker, using ourselves as an instrument of portal openings? Here are some suggestions I offer you in joining the symphony of sound:

- Don't judge yourself … but push beyond your natural hesitation to use your voice. Hum or speak the words to an inspirational song playing in the background, even for a breath or two.

- Record your voice chanting, speaking, humming and listen back for feedback. But, remember! It is not exactly your voice – because we are resonance chambers and the recorder squashes our tone.

- If you cringe, hearing that you are out of tune or feel wobbly inside from the skewed vibration with your 'melody' then turn up a song playing in the background and begin again to follow their lead. Eventually we resonate. It takes practice. Practice in the car. Practice in the shower.

- Start silently and then use your voice for a breath sequence such as, "Take one or two deep breaths and relax into this healing space". Once you start speaking, you will eventually find it easier to continue.

- Speak when you invite in a Being of Love and Light: "I call upon the Healing Angels for this beloved soul for their intent of …". Eventually you might add a sentence before or after.

- Use your voice at the end of the session to bring your client back to 3D. Ask them to move their hands and feet, to bring their consciousness to their eyes, to breathe 3 times. State that you are sealing in the healing. Sometimes, after getting used to using your voice in the end of a session it is not so hard to add the beginning.

- Feel comfortable with the client's Invited Guests. We sometimes feel constrained with vocally stating our own Guide set if we are unsure how the client will handle hearing it stated. Spend a few minutes beforehand with a new client determining their cosmology.

- Don't judge yourself (multiple reminders :); love yourself into using your vocal instrument.

Conductor, Conduct!

With a client on the table, and their eyes closed, feel free to channel the Inner Maestro and conduct the orchestra! Like any good Conductor, use your hands, move your body, feel the music and free the instruments to soar into their perfection.

In beginning your Prayer of Intent:

- Draw your Reiki symbols on you
- Draw the symbols on your client
- Draw the symbols on the ceiling and in the room
- Move with your breath and the symbols

While inviting Guests to come:

- Open your arms wide, palms up, inviting those Higher Beings in
- Motion to the client's 7th chakra as you call in their Soul and their Highest Self
- Motion vertically upwards if you call upon their I Am or Angelic lineage
- Motion in a sweeping arm pattern if you invite in their Guides, Angels, Teachers, and Loved Ones of the Light

When suggesting 3 conscious breaths, in the beginning and/or at the end of a session:

- Above their bodies, trace the breath from their head to their toes

- Stand below their feet and motion in the cords from their soles of their feet to the earth

When opening the 7th chakra to higher vibrations:

- Stand near the top of their head and motion upwards as if you are tracing the branches and trunk of their human/angelic tree

While saying your Guided Visualization, motion your arms:

- Make an arch when you describe a circular doorway or Archway of Flowers
- Step forward when you invite them to
- If offering or receiving a gift from Spirit, open your arms and hands to receive and to give a gift

When finishing a session:

- Move from head to foot to clear and align energies

Using a Crystal 'Baton'

A conductor uses a baton so that all in the orchestra can see and follow the rhythm in complete unison. It sometimes seems like a magic wand the way each conductor weaves their spell, to leave us spellbound. In our work, many energy healers enjoy using crystals. Weave your crystalline spell.

I have a few different types of crystal 'wands' or long, cylindrical crystals, which I sometimes use in sessions. It is fun to use it as an actual 'baton', waving it to the beat of the song, whether the song is my Prayer of Intent, or an actual song that I sing for them.

Crystals can be wonderful tools for energy healers and there is much to read up on the subject. You can also follow your intuition and be guided to a crystal that calls to you.

- Use your crystal to draw symbols on the client and room

- Hold your crystal to magnify and enhance your intuitive gifts (especially clear quartz)

- Place your crystal on the table, next to your client's chakra or the body area you are focusing upon

- Touch all 10 of your fingertips lightly with the tip of your crystal to assist your 'tracking' or sensing abilities

- Tap the tip of your crystal to your 6th or brow chakra, or, lightly touch a circlet on your crown chakra. This opens you up to higher wisdom and connections

- Hold your crystal and visualize the tip touching the bottoms of your 10 toes to anchor you more firmly as a healer stepping through portals and dimensions

Remember to clear your crystals before and after sessions. Do this with breath, water, salt, soil, sun, moon, breath, Reiki symbols, or intent.

Musical Reprise

I design Prayers of Intent and Guided Visualizations for both the beginnings and endings of sessions. These serve as functioning escalators, bringing both me and my client up to multidimensional space, and then back again to 3D reality, feeling safe, grounded, vital, and secure.

If you have a particular visualization and have taken your client to a sacred space, bring them back. This can be done fairly simply by reversing the trajectory. I usually do the return journey more quickly than the time I invested bringing them there. We are used to waking up from dream states. A short period of re-entry is usually all that is needed to begin the final integration process.

Going on our Journey:

> *"We find ourselves walking through a colorful meadow on a beautiful day. The sun is shining, and we are walking on a path of rainbow colored rocks. Up ahead there is an Archway of Flowers. You have been here before. You know this is a sacred space and as we pass under the Arch we pass into the Sacred Grove. Hear the melodic rhythm of the gentle waterfall as it calls to you to come and rest for a while."*

> *"You see a small waterfall emptying into a little pond. There are rocks there for you to sit on, to lay on if you wish. You can put your feet in the water or even jump right in. You can walk along the back of the Waterfall and see the rainbow colors emerge from the water and sunlight."*

> *"You realize you are not alone. There are Beings of Love and Light who come to visit you!'* (continue)

Coming back from our Journey:

> *"We are now going to make our way back from this Sacred Grove.*

> *Follow the rainbow rock pathway back to the Archway of Flowers, back to this room, back to your body, back to your breath.*

> *Follow your breath down your legs and feet, into the earth. Feel safe, secure, and full of energy."*

Trust yourself. You are a perfectly attuned instrument, a veritable chamber orchestra of one (One). You are a dedicated professional and have invested years (lifetimes) in this pursuit, otherwise you would not be reading these words!

To help jumpstart your own melodies, chants, and inspirations, we offer you samples of our own, in the following chapter.

Chapter 4

Vocal Harmonics

This chapter offers the lyrics to Arise Harmonics – songs chanted and sung before, during, and at the close of sessions. Feel free to take from these words those that touch your heart for either Prayers of Intent or for Guided Visualizations.

Songs for beginning a session are detailed here. Songs for the middle of healing sessions can be found in Part 3, Prayers of Intent. The final group, ending songs, can be found in Part 4, Guided Visualizations. The full list is detailed below.

To hear the melodies for these expressions, search Lorelynn Mirage Cardo under www.Youtube.com and www.TonyCardomusic.com.

Songs and Chants to Begin Healing Sessions

Elorhaim Seraphim Magnificat & Isola

In Waters Deep

Fractal Curves

Please, Sing Me Rhymes

Songs and Chants for Middle of Healing Sessions

   Within Your Eyes

   Opening

   Overlighting Angels

   Instant Replay

   The Right Time

   Land of a Dreamer

   Melody

Songs and Chants to Ending Healing Sessions

   Freedom Song

   Beacon in the Storm

   Downpour

   We Are Complete

   Open Angel Wings

Elorhaim Seraphim Magnificat

Elorhaim

Seraphim

Magnificat

(Note: This is my personal SoulAnge Harmonic or Soul Ray name. I have a simple melody to sing my name which comes from The Song of Creation angelic lineage. This song immediately elevates me to a higher vibrational state.)

Isola

Isola

Isola

Isola

Radiant

One

Isola

Isola

Isola

Fearless One

Blazing

Loving

Eternal

One!

(Note: This is a Soul based calling for my clients. As I begin a session and sing this loving chant, I put Reiki symbols above their field and on each of their chakras.)

In Waters Deep

Help me please
I'm on my knees
Hear my pleas
Have mercy

On stormy seas and wintry freeze
Help me release
Furies, juries, humilities
Guilties, haunting injuries
Don't want to flee
And hide in my stories
On bended knees
I'm begging please
Thru unknown seas
I now release

Beloved, please
Come to me in my need
Let me see myself in Your Beauty
And know what can be
Let me see myself
And know True Reality
In Your Glory

On gentle seas and summery breeze
Soothe me with rhythmic breathes
Thank you for the keys
Unlocking old beliefs

I see through the weeds
to
Crystalline Clarity
Heartfelt Ease
Highest destiny

Opening Quantum Doorways

We breathe into our sublimity
Throughout infinity

In waters deep
We swim and leap
Thru inner seas
And true inner sees
In our dailies

Eternal journeys
Help me see
Help me know
Help me live
Help me breath
Your Glory
My Glory
Our Glory

(Note: This song is wonderful for yourself or for clients who are experiencing challenges, both positive and negative. Allow the timbre of your voice to hold the vibrations of the pleas.)

Fractal Curves

To practice the art of healing
Find a path thru the pain
Follow the changing fractal curves
And encounter wholeness again

To practice the art of loving
Find a path thru the loss
Follow the unchanging fractal curves
And enter without remorse

To practice the art of living
Find a path thru the changes
Dance with the spiraling fractals
And be embraced again and again

Fractal Curves
Patterns merge
Patterns swerve
They submerge
And re-emerge
Till they are purged
Our patterns serve!

To practice the art of breathing
Find a path to the Divine
Follow the thread of compassion
Merging Heart and Infinite Mind

Patterns unfold
Inner worlds behold
We stand at the threshold
Untold
Re-souled

76

Opening Quantum Doorways

De-coded
The Eternal Fractal Scroll

To practice the art of healing, loving, living, breathing
Unfold
Enfold
Within our Fractal Gold

(Note: This song illumines the patterns in our lives, which unfold as fractals in multi-dimensions. We untangle and reweave harmonic patterns with this song.)

Please, Sing Me Rhymes

Please

> *As I'm on the ocean*
> *I'm in need*
> *Longing for devotion*
> *On your wings*
> *I need to fly*
> *And I don't need to wonder why*
> *I have*
> *Another day to know you*
> *Another day to keep on loving you*

Please

> *Never let me lose the joy of life*
> *Another kind of journey*
> *Where I scale the mountain high*
> *And I don't need to wonder why*
> *I have*
> *Another way to know you*
> *Another way to keep on loving you*

Please

> *Let me know*
> *My heart is so afraid of letting go*

Please

> *Sing me rhymes*
> *In the middle of night*
> *And when another morning breaks*
> *I feel the warmth of your embrace*
> *I'll play my part*
> *I'll sing your Song of Love*

Please
> *Give me all the strength*
> *To see me through*
> *I never want to lose you*
> *For this time we can begin*
> *The sound of love is on the wind*
> *It moves the clouds above me*
> *It moves my life forever*
> *Close to you*

Music and lyrics by Tony Cardo

Part 3

Prayers

of

Intent

Chapter 5

Step One: The Invitation

Party Planning

When we want to host a party, there are a few steps we take before the fun begins. First, what type of party are we thinking of, is there a theme or purpose?

Next, who should we invite for the best outcome? Is this a party for a specific person, like a birthday, or a party honoring an event, like a holiday or anniversary? Is it a family party with relatives and a large home cooked meal? Or, is it a party for a birthday girl's friends with games and toys? As good party planners know, there's a lot of behind the scenes work before the invitations go out!

Being the oldest of my siblings, close cousins, and our neighborhood friends, I was very familiar with the general birthday party progression – dressing up fancy, running around, pin the tail on the donkey games, opening presents, singing Happy Birthday, blowing out candles, eating cake and ice cream, and then running around some more until the party ended.

For my 10th birthday, my Mom invited a handful of my friends from school to come to my house for my party, without younger siblings or parents in tow. I put on a fancy birthday dress and expectantly waited for my friends to arrive.

Just before they arrived, the thought struck me: "What are we going to do -- what if it's boring?" And, like the Law of Attraction (I now know so well), I remember the party being disappointing, boring, and over pretty early. The guests sulked. There were no games, no running around. The cake, presents, and singing 'Happy Birthday' was no big deal. There were no little kids to be entertained with.

I was clearly out of my element and realized a little too late that the birthday party game format had changed, and I wasn't prepared. At one point, I ran to my Mom in the kitchen and complained to her that it was boring, and we had nothing to do! My Mom, her hands full with younger children and her own chores, exasperatingly said, "Well, Do something then!" It was my last planned birthday party until 50 :)

Taking the spooky and, even, the sacred elements away from our work, for a moment, we could consider Prayer of Intent and Guided Visualizations, and the entire healing session, as parts of one big party.

Planning and intent helps (Prayer of Intent).

Know your guest of honor (Client and their cosmology and intention).

Know which guests to invite (the Guides you call upon).

Determine the appropriate games (Guided Visualizations).

This fore-planning helps you host a wonderful experience. As I had to learn the hard way, you, the party planner, need to track and respond to the party scene for the best possible outcome. Spontaneity is intuitive and wonderful. But, I would recommend spontaneity after some planning.

Healing shifts, movement of stuck energies, connection with the Divine, increasing intuitive gifts, clarity, courage and rededication – these and more are all the presents available to both us and to the 'birthday girl or boy'.

Segment Intending

Esther Hicks and Abraham (www.abraham-hicks.com) are the premiere troubadours of Law of Attraction and its various component parts. Ask and It Is Given, their first book, is a staple and foundation of energy work, and of having a successful party (life).

They offer a number of exercises designed to help you move from an unwanted place to one of joy, excitement and creation. I could have used this knowledge for my 10th birthday party.

Segment Intending is one of these exercises. What do you want to have happen for this minute? Or, this minute? Or this one? Perhaps in your car, thoughts a-popping, you need to get food for dinner. Abraham advises breaking down the shopping trip to small segments of time.

In the car:

> "I intend this drive to be safe and relaxing."

In the parking lot:

> "The perfect parking spot is ready and waiting for me."

In the store:

> "I get great ideas for tonight's meal when I see the produce and protein selections."

> "I love to cook for my family."

> "I love buying healthy foods for my loved ones."

At the cashier counter:

> "I have all the time I need to wait for my turn at the counter."

> "I trust that my money covers everything I need or want."

> "The Universe is lavish Abundance. I am a child of the Universe. Abundance is my birthright. I am grateful to pay for this bounty. Thank you!"

On the drive home:

> "I trust that I got everything I need. If not, then the meal will be surprising and healthy both!"

> "Taking in all the groceries is good exercise for my heart, lungs, and arm muscles. If I get help, so much the better!"

As you can see, if you Segment Intend, even with 1 or 2 of those thoughtful intents crossing your mind, you find that you are now consciously creating your life, your thoughts (not easy to do), your fears (even harder to control), and your activities.

As opposed to dashing into the car, driving like a maniac to the store, yelling (or wanting to yell) at someone for taking 'your' parking space, frantically running up and down aisles throwing food in your cart, slamming home, exhausted, and, perhaps, angry or overwhelmed at the specter of carrying in, unpacking and putting bags of groceries away, and, then, cooking for a hungry family.

Segment Intending offers opportunities for us to be mindful, grateful, in conscious and creative control of our life activities. It also helps confront auto-pilot thought and fear loops. It takes a lot of practice, but it is worth it.

Prayer of Intent is similar, and yet different.

Prayer of Intent for Yourself and for Others

Prayers of Intent set the stage for healing work and for moving consciously throughout our day. They are more expansive than Segment Intending, as we are consciously framing an event, not just a moment or segment of our time.

Both are important tools for us as Lightworkers, but we need only say one Prayer of Intent for ourselves or our client, rather than break the time period into tiny segments. It is similar to my writing these words to you on my computer. I need both my large muscle groups as well as my fine motor coordination to sit here on this beautiful day, typing, and sharing my thoughts and experiences with you. Both are needed.

You can Segment Intend throughout your day, especially during stressful times, so that you are aware of the day-to-day steps you take in this precious lifetime. You can also say a Prayer of Intent for yourself for an issue or concern you are having, such as a Prayer of Intent for Abundance, for a Healthy Relationship, for a Wonderful, Creative, Respectful Work Environment, or for a Radiantly Healthy Body. The topics are as endless as our thoughts and desires. The Prayer can be one you write up and say every day until movement occurs. Remember, Law of Attraction and our vibrational set point.

What you need to be aware of, when you design a Prayer of Intent for your own concerns or for a client, is to be pristine that you do not impinge upon another's free will choices! More about this is written in Book 6 of the Tools for Lightworkers Series, the Reiki 1 and 2 Manual.

We have the tools to go beyond time, space and dimension with Reiki 2 symbols (Hon Sha Ze Sho Nen, the distance sending symbol). We also design Prayers of Intent for ourselves and others. What is harder to understand is that we do not have the ethical responsibility to send to another person's life choices, unless they are our child, under 18 years of age or someone who is under our power of attorney and who cannot make their life decisions. That is, unless someone specifically asks us to intervene!

For example, you design a Prayer of Intent for your Soul Mate to come to you now. This is an appropriate prayer for you to make. However, if you know someone who you think, believe, hope, intuit, feel with all your might, is your Soul Mate, you still have no business intending them in your Prayer of Intent.

You may intend "Someone like (Your Companion) who is kind, caring, funny, and generous" and then add "Highest and Greatest Good for All". This is appropriate.

Intending that "(Your Companion) opens to the love that we share throughout all time" is sweet and romantic, but it is NOT something that is put in a Prayer of Intent. Be pristine in your work!

Also, I caution against 'psychic snooping' of any kind. "What is (Your Companion) really feeling about me?" is not something you should entertain, either for yourself, or to answer a client's plea. Even if you do get intimations, intuitions, visions, knowings, especially if you get intimations, intuitions, visions, knowings, don't decrease your gift orders by this well- meant peeking in!

Design the Invitation

The first step is to invite Spirit to be with us for the healing and em-powering session. Like our party invitation, Who are you inviting?

It can be as simple as calling upon

> Healing Angels
>
> God, Source, Creator
>
> Jesus
>
> Reiki Masters
>
> The Client's Soul, Higher Self, or Guardian Angel

To broaden the invitation, I often invite in a phalanx of healers, like a medical theatre. It is soothing and opens pathways to your intuitive gifts and quantum space when you consciously call Beings of Love and Light to the healing space you are opening.

By invoking these Beings, you are stepped, effortlessly, into multidimensional space.

When your client hears you invite these Beings, they are given the subtext message that they can relax into the healing experience and trust what is happening. Most importantly, they know they are safe and are invited into multidimensional space as they hear that you are verbally and consciously inviting in Spiritual Luminaries to be present. You might also invite their Loved Ones of the Light. Sometimes, this invitation alone is enough to begin shifting energies within them for a healing to occur.

Take a breath and pace yourself through this beginning phase of invitation. You don't want to minimize your invitation, but you don't need to invite 'everyone'. For a party, you know not every guest is the best choice for the optimal purpose of the party. If you are hosting a 4th birthday party for your child, you choose guests differently than you would for a 4th of July barbeque. The same applies to the healing 'party'.

Begin to center and inspire yourself, maybe with sage or candles. Silently ask for help. Draw Reiki symbols on yourself – especially Mastery symbols if you have been attuned to Reiki Master. Draw symbols in the 4 corners of your room. Sing your Angelic Soul Ray name and lineage.

Get Guests' Addresses (Opening Quantum Doorways)

Do you have all the correct addresses? Where does the Buddha live? Or Archangel Michael? Are you sending to the correct address?

This is a huge quantum leap in our understanding and in our daily practice. For millennia, we have been conditioned to believe we are not worthy to invoke the Divine. Only intermediaries such as priests, ministers, saints, martyrs, Jesus, oracles, shamans normally do this work.

We have also been conditioned to believe that we are children, sinners, or lost orphans of the universe, a cosmic crap shoot, a joke.

That is why Parts 1 and 2 of this book are important to synthesize. Because, now, WE are the ones calling in the Divine.

We offer the invitation.

We accept Their RSVP.

We open the door and usher Them in.

We set the stage of what is intended.

We dialogue back and forth with our Guests.

We offer to be the go-between, if necessary, for our client with these most sublime Visitors.

We host the party, from beginning to end.

WE do all this!

Can you do this? Yes!

If I can, you can. If you want to, you can.

How can you possibly do all this?

By practice. By allowing. By asking.

Be the host, even with a Guest Who might overwhelm you with their luminosity. Be as polite and generous as you would with a friend we might invite out of compassion.

This is working within the Quantum … there are jumps from level to level. We don't need to force or pull anything. We invite. There is an opening. Guest(s) arrive.

Exciting Challenges

How do we determine Who to invite, perceive correctly that Guests are present, discern Who is there, and listen, intuitively, to get clear messages?

This calls upon our higher gift orders,

clairvoyance (clear seeing),

clairaudience (clear hearing),

clairsentience (clear feeling), and

claircognizance (clear thinking).

The most common question energy healers ask: "How can I increase my higher gifts, so I can dialogue with Spirit?"

Answer, practice! With sincerity and purity of purpose.

And, consider Book 5 of the Tools for Lightworkers Series, The Lightworker Manual. We offer Lightworker Apprentice programs from introductory to advanced levels and the Manual reflects this.

Another challenge is determining how to report to the client what has been said or done by our Guests during the session.

This is a very subtle yet important consideration!

Are you sure that you are 100% correct in getting this multidimensional information?

Are you 100% sure that you are getting information from, for example, Archangel Michael vs. your imagination of what Archangel Michael would say?

Can we ever get 100% certitude? In the quantum probability universe?

Finally, if we do feel that we are correct in our receiving the information and interpreting it, are we 100% sure that we are to give this information to the client?

There is tremendous responsibility in doing this work!

We must be pristine in our integrity and our desire to open quantum doorways and bring forth connections and information for ourselves and our clients.

You might choose to be silent with intuitive communication and work internally with the Guides without bringing the information forward to your client. Some healers do. Alternatively, I have known healers who repeat everything that comes into their head, with the (possibly mistaken?) belief that "if they hear it, they say it", without any filter.

Because, "Who am I to censor Spirit?"

Interesting question. But, wrongly asked.

Who are we to censor Spirit? WE are the ones saying we are in direct contact with the Divine. We are the ones, for many of our clients, who are standing in the stead of oracles, shamans, mediums, ministers, and Jesus!

This is a path that you must navigate if you wish to do the work. Be immaculate in following your guidance.

My advice:

"Be humble in the face of Infinity!"

Walk nimbly, carefully, honestly, with integrity and, especially, with compassion. Invite. Dialogue. And, then, take responsibility for what you are going to do in the client's field and what you are going to tell the client. Be responsible, because you are responsible! If you do not act in 100% integrity, you will be stepped out of this energy. This is not about ego- gifts but about being part of a benevolent, multidimensional team!

To be able to do this work is a privilege and an honor. Be pristine.

Visualize the Invisible

A mudra is a hand gesture that informs or enhances sacred space and sacred energy flows. Consider how non-verbals enhance our verbal communications. Shaking our head up and down to signify 'yes'. Shrugging our shoulders up to our ears to indicate 'not sure' or 'who knows?'

For the Invitation, using hand gestures helps me visualize the invisible. For each session, I:

> open my arms wide to begin the invocation of calling in Creator Source energies
>
> motion to the top of the client's crown chakra as I invite in their Soul, their Highest and Greatest Self
>
> motion vertically above their head as I call upon their I AM Presence
>
> and, start at the left of their head and open an arc or half circle around the client as I call in the Masters, Teachers, Guides and Loved Ones of the Light

In these few gestures and words, I have set up a room full of wonderful energies to begin the 2nd part of Prayers of Intent, *The Purpose*. Why are we all gathered here? What is the client's intent? This is a free will universe. We are there to set the stage. What does the client intend?

Words are power, and they define our reality.

For healers and energy workers, verbalizing our intent serves us and serves the client in many ways. It is first and foremost a sacred tool allowing us to enter sacred space where we are empowered to alter 'reality' and bring healing and empowerment to the situation.

Guided Visualizations, the next energy tool discussed in this book, allows us to 'see' and 'cross' into invisible space. Current academic cosmologists and astrophysicists who theorize multiple dimensions state that we are existing right now in 10 or 11 dimensions. If you study their work, they visualize these dimensions as mathematical or geometric models.

Brian Greene, a favorite cosmologist of mine, believes we can understand multiple dimensions with the imagery of an ant who is crawling across a telephone wire that is made of many interweaving strands. The ant can't see or understand what is happening, she is just crawling, to the best of her ability, across the telephone pole to get to the other side. The ant doesn't know anything about the wires, how they work or why they work. Ants don't even, from their perspective, know there are multiple wires. They are just inching their way forward.

Interesting perspective, but one that does not take into account that we are co-creators. When we open multidimensional doorways, WE OPEN them. We are the conscious creators. We increase our 'clair' skills to work in the quantum. And, we respect the medium as well as respecting ourselves and our clients, wherever they are in their process.

In this way, we make the invisible visible, we work within the infinite probability of the quantum. We do this for ourselves and if they wish, we do this for our clients, so they can step forward and set a frequency of healing and wholeness for themselves.

Step One: The Invitation

1. Begin with the highest energies of your model of reality. You can start with Creator, God, Goddess, All There Is – whatever names you use comfortably to access the name for the unnamable, ineffable, all pervasive intelligence.

> List some names that you feel comfortable calling upon and some personal words that you can use to open your sacred space.

2. Call upon the Luminous Beings who you are aligned with: Jesus, Ascended Masters, Angels, etc. Who is the client aligned with? What issue is the client intending healing or information? That will inform Who you are inviting.

> List Luminous Beings you would like to call upon for your healing sessions:

3. You might call upon qualities of Love and Light, Clarity, Abundance, Peace as energetic resonances rather than the Angels and Guides who work in these are. Or, you might call upon Devic or Earth based energies. This depends upon your client's intent and your expansion of their intent.

   List any Qualities you wish to call upon:

4. Call upon your client's soul to be present and the Masters, Teachers, Guides, Angels and Loved Ones of the Light who work with your client to be present for the session.

   Practice inviting in Others:

5. Call upon your soul and your higher I AM lineage. This immediately steps you into quantum-scapes.

   Practice naming yourself and your Soul lineages:

Lists of possible Party Guests and Medical Team members can be found in Chapter 2 as well as in Book 4, of the Tools for Lightworkers Series, Dialogue with Spirit.

My Invitation

I call upon the Creator and the Forces of Love and Light.

I call upon the Soul and Highest Self of (Client's name) and the Masters, Teachers and Loved Ones of the Light for this Beloved.

I call upon the Elorhaim Seraphim Magnificat, Song of Creation, energies to be present (my SoulAnge Harmonic lineage).

I call upon Jesus, Mary, and the Bodhisattvas throughout time to be present here for this healing (state intent).

I fill this space completely with:

> *Divine Love and Wisdom* (as I draw the Reiki Cho Ku Rei symbol in the room over the client)

> *Mental and Emotional healing, balance and empowerment* (as I draw the Reiki Sei He Ki symbol in the room over the client)

> *The ability to cross between time, space and dimension to set healing and empowering energies for (client's name) (as I draw the Reiki Hon Sha Ze Sho Nen symbol in the room over the client)*

> *And affirm they stand as a master in this world today. (If the client is a Reiki Master, of if I feel mastery energies will enhance the session, I draw one or both of Reiki Master symbols over the client.)*

Then, I begin to state

Part 2: The Purpose and conclude with

Part 3: The Setting of protections and conditions.

Design Your Unique Prayer of Intent
Step 1: The Invitation

Write a sample Prayer of Intent, Step 1: The Invitation. Use your creativity, your heart, your soul, and maybe some poetry or something that makes you smile inwardly or outwardly. Play with this.

Version 1:

Version 2:

Chapter 6

Step Two: The Purpose

What, exactly, are you doing during the session?

Is it a general Reiki energy healing session? You still might want to ask the client if there is anything they wish to focus upon. Many times, the client does not have anything in particular they want to focus on, or they have trouble defining what they want. This is a very important part of the healing session for your client.

We do not 'do' the healing!

We, as healers, are the ones who set the stage and bear witness with them. We can accelerate the forces of healing, love and light by our presence, our intent, our vibratory frequency, but they are the ones responsible for their own healing. It is important that the client be able to rise to the healing energies.

Broaden and Define

As we are the Conductor of this healing Orchestra, it is a joy for us to help shape the verbal languaging of client intent. We are opening specific doorways in the quantum and dialoguing with Guides of Love and Light as to specific outcomes and information.

Honor your client's request and then consider expanding upon it if their request is too narrow, for example, if they say their "knee hurts". Or, define with them the intent if their request is, "Oh, whatever" (common response).

For a hurt knee you could ask for

> *"(Client) is requesting healing for her knee and, also, for balance in the world as she confidently walks forward on her highest destiny path".*

For "oh, whatever" a little talk beforehand would help you define more of their intent. Perhaps they would align with:

> *"We are intending that this Beloved feel abundant in all ways and has joy in her everyday precious moments".*

Or,

> *"(Client) intends to feel secure and inspired in moving forward as a Reiki healer, offering her dedicated service to increase Light, Love and Compassion on our precious planet."*

Or,

> *"(Client) is intending to step forth as a master energy, so much needed and appreciated at this time. Blessings and appreciation for undertaking this journey!"*

Check with your client, before you say the Prayer of Intent, before you broaden or define their request. Ask if this sounds good to them. Although this might take a few minute's discussion to get clarity on the intent, it is very important from the view of the healing paradigm.

The client needs to take responsibility for the healing.

If they wish to contact a specific Being, such as a family member who has passed, a past life, or the karmic reasoning behind a current situation, I make effort to work within the quantum for their request. I call upon their Beloved to be present.

If they wish information on an event in their lives, I might call upon 'Those Who Hold the Records' (which is my way of getting past life or archetypal information).

I call upon their Soul for Soul Contract information.

However, I always let the client know beforehand that I set the condition, 'Highest and Greatest Good for All' for the session. This means that, if a Being comes to the session and I get a message for them, that is the highest and greatest good. If they don't come or if I don't get any message, then *that* is the highest and greatest good. I don't promise.

And, most importantly, make a subtle reminder to your client that *THEY* will get information either on the table during our session or later, throughout the day, during their night's sleep, or in the near future. The message and connection can come to them directly, rather than through you as intermediary. We all are Co-Creators.

Practice Broadening

Louise Hay's Heal Your Life is a great distillation of many physical dis-eases and body organs, and their possible mental, emotional, and spiritual correlates. You can also google online for the spiritual messages behind certain dis-eases. And, read up a little on the client's area of concern in case you get messages, pictures or diagrams during the session; this way, you can interpret them correctly.

For example, let us envision a client coming to see you for an energy healing session for the following concerns. The mental/emotional background and affirmation from Louise Hay's Heal Your Life would help me consider broadening as follows.

Diabetes

> 'Deep sorrow. No sweetness left. Longing for what might have been. A great need to control.' (Hay)

> Prayer of Intent Step 2: The Purpose

> *"We call upon the Universal Mother, the One who nurtures, embraces, and gives to all, to be present for the Beloved in her healing of diabetes fully and completely so that she may enjoy the sweetness of this precious life and of every life circumstance. We intend to honor all our life choices, even the hard ones and trust that we are following our destiny of light!"*

Chronic pain   'Guilt seeking punishment. Need to release the past.' (Hay)

Prayer of Intent Step 2: The Purpose

"We call upon God, the Angels and Archangels, especially Archangel Raphael who works with healing all physical, mental and emotional pain, to be here today for (Client) to release her from karmic debt. It is full and complete. She is now intent on stepping forth on her path with ease, comfort, joy, and compassion for herself and all others. "

Loss of job   Prayer of Intent Step 2: The Purpose

"I call upon Archangel Michael to be present for (Client) as he releases all that is appropriate to let go of at this moment in time. This stage in his Hero's Journey of working for (company name or occupational title) is full and complete. We trust in the goodness of life and the infinite abundance of the Universe to provide opportunities for more growth, more joy, more connection, and a stronger commitment to our Highest Destiny life path."

Practice Defining

Feeling of being overwhelmed

Prayer of Intent, Step 2: The Purpose

"I call upon Jesus, Mary, and the Forces of Love and Light to be present for this Beloved Being as she breathes in wisdom, acceptance, allowance, and appropriate action. She breathes out all that can be released, trusting that this is a Universe based upon free will and benevolence. (Client) breathes in unconditional love and support. And, she breathes out her wisdom, her experience, her joys and lessons so that her Light might shine up and down her DNA lineage."

Increasing Intuitive Gifts

Prayer of Intent, Step 2: The Purpose

"Welcome, Beings of Love and Light! Those who hold the Records for this Beloved Being, known to us as (Name). She is intending to open widely her intuitive gifts, especially (name the gift, ex. clairvoyance). I call upon (Client's) Soul, her Highest Self, and the Soul Contracts that are in place this lifetime as she intends to increase seeing Spirit manifest in her life and in service to her clients. I also call upon Archangel Metatron for underlying spiritual knowledge and St. Germaine for overarching healing techniques."

Wanting a Relationship

Prayer of Intent, Step 2: The Purpose

"I call upon Quan Yin, the Goddess of Mercy and Compassion to be present for (Client) and help us all beam love, connection, mercy and compassion upon her Inner Child and in her life to-day. I call upon Archangel Chamuel to be present to work with her on her Soul Mate path, aligning to love, joyful longing, and exciting expectations."

The ability to broaden or define what the client intends involves your working on an intuitive level. Don't rely on your past experience, or assume you have an answer for them. Be open to higher guidance for your client and the situation.

Perhaps you have dealt with a similar situation and the ways and means you used to bring yourself back into balance seem the right way for your client to try. You certainly may share your experience with them, but I strongly recommend that you speak from your experience while you are sitting together in chairs, before the healing, checking in.

Once the client gets on the table, lying down in a vulnerable position, listening to you calling in Jesus and their Angels, what you say takes on another dimension. Your client is more sensitive and receptive on a deeper level than a conversation, advice-giving talk. Be careful and cautious in your communications once you begin the healing sequences and Prayer of Intent.

As we understand each person is unique, so too each manifestation of dis-ease is unique as well. This became very clear to me when I first began my etheric healing work. I needed to offer 30 sessions and get detailed feedback from clients. Within that group, I had three people ask me to work on their knees!

Louise Hay mentions knees signify pride, ego, and inability to give in. Although this might be the generalized meaning, be open to your intuition during the Prayer of Intent for unique prayers for each client.

Surprisingly, I found that each of the three sessions on knee pain involved different chakras and different underlying stories.

One related to a feeling of sibling rivalry between herself and her brother. He had a life of luxury and she worked hard to survive, which she felt was unfair. The block was lodged in her 3rd chakra, the solar plexus. This 'weighed' her down and unbalanced her.

The second one experienced a death of an adult child and was literally on his knees in grief. This death was beaming from his 4th, heart chakra, and his 2nd, sacral or relationship chakra.

The third client needed to move forward in her life after midlife changes. She had a nasty divorce and felt scarcity, remorse, and anger. She never was able to express her emotions about the unfair distribution of their marital assets (he hid and kept them all). This information was stored in her 5th chakra.

Knees are traditionally associated with the 1st chakra. All had relief from our work together (See Book 10 of the Tools for Lightworkers Series, Spectrum Energetics for more of these case studies).

So, don't assume. Be accessible, uncluttered, and unshuttered to the information as it comes to you during the session. We so much desire to help that we sometimes skip ahead of ourselves. Trust that the unique information for that person and that situation will come.

Design Your Unique Prayer of Intent,
Step 2: The Purpose

Write a sample Prayer of Intent, Step 2: The Purpose. Choose a topic or follow my suggestions: abundance and feelings of lack, desperately want a child, don't feel as smart or as successful as others, want to start a healing practice.

Version 1:

Version 2:

Chapter 7

Step Three: The Ending

The final step in your Prayer of Intent is to end by setting protections and conditions.

There are many ways to do this!

- State that you are protected and safe
- Fill your space with Reiki symbols and words
- Put white light in the corners of your room
- Burn Sage for blessings and protections

Wrap a Blanket of Safety Over the Client

It is good to set a protective space around yourself and your client when you enter multidimensional space. We are traveling. We want to intend safety.

You might say,

> *"Archangel Michael, please bring your Host of Angels here at this time to this place for (Client) so that we are in Love and Light."*

> *"I call upon all that is Holy and Sacred to be present and seal this sacred space and this sacred work."*

> *"I affirm that we (you and Client) are in the right place, at the right time, doing all the right things. Thank you for Your Protection."*

> *"(Client) affirms that she is intending only good to come from this intervention, both for herself and for her loved ones. She releases all to Love and Light."*

My Envelope of Safety:

> *"I affirm that we are in safe and protected sacred space"*

> (At the same time as I am saying these words, I draw the Reiki Power symbol, Cho Ku Rei, on the four corners of the ceiling and a large on in the room.)

State Conditions

What conditions do you have for the session? This refers to a previous discussion about agenda and accepting free will choices. It is perfectly acceptable to intend for a client, "perfect and radiant health and wellness". Then I would add my condition.

My condition:

"Highest and Greatest Good for All"

Stating this condition covers anything that can occur with the healing. 'Highest and greatest good' puts a block on any personal agenda you or your client might hold. We wish to have healings occur exactly as the client intends, but, it might not, in their highest and greatest good, end the way we both wish. This short phrase allows for both will and surrender.

Consider: Would you want an outcome that was not your highest and greatest good? Something very important to reflect upon.

Consider: If it is highest and greatest good for one person, then it is highest and greatest good for everyone, including you and those beings who are in relation to the client, including their bodily systems.

Consider: It is highest and greatest good for whatever Beings of Love and Light arrive and dialogue with us for the session (or not). We can trust that.

Other conditions you might like to try:

"Bring Light to this healing and to every occurrence that arises from this session."

"I affirm everything that happens as a result of this healing session is in accordance with Divine Will"

"May only Love and Light follow you as you follow your inner dreams and your outer goals."

"Peace, serenity and clarity follow us every day in every way."

109

Politely End

Signal to your client, to your Invited Guests, and to yourself that the Prayer of Intent is completed and you are moving onto another part of the healing session, especially Guided Visualizations.

My Ending:

"So Be It"

You might consider:

"Amen"

"Blessings!" (is a favorite of many).

"Namaste" (is another well- known phrase, especially in yoga circles).

"In Lak'esh" (is Mayan for 'I am another yourself', similar to Namaste).

"Thank You."

Design Your Unique Prayer of Intent, Step 3: The Ending

Write a sample Prayer of Intent, Step 3: The Ending.

Practice designing a few ways to end your Prayer of Intent. Set your protections and conditions.

Version 1:

Version 2:

Sample Prayers of Intent

Below are a number of Prayers of Intent with spaces between the steps.

Prayer of Intent to Prepare Offering
Energy Healing Sessions

I call upon the Creator and the Forces of Love and Light

I call upon Jesus, Mary, and the Magdala, Tower of Strength energies

I call upon the Angels and Archangels of healing and enlightenment especially Archangel Michael, Archangel Raphael, and Archangel Uriel.

I call upon my Soul, my Highest and Greatest Self and the Teachers, Masters, Guides and Loved Ones of the Light to be with me today.

I affirm and intend to walk my Highest Destiny path and ask to be guided effortlessly and joyfully on my steps today. Thank you for each Magnificent Being of Love and Light who comes to me today.

I affirm that everything that happens today is the Highest and Greatest Good for All.

So be it. Amen.

Prayer of Intent for Help with Family and Loved Ones

I recognize you (family member and relationship to you) as a

powerful, infinite, magnificent Being of Love and Light

> *Who has chosen*

> *On A Soul Level!*

> *This particular life path*

I accept and honor your free will Soul Choices!

Please help my Beloved One

As they work their way through (............ remember to define, broaden, look for the gifts in the condition).

In the Highest and Greatest Good for All

Amen.

Prayer of Intent for Help with Physical Distress

Quan Yin, The Goddess of Mercy, She Who hears the pleas of this world, please hear my pleas!

Please help me hear and understand the messages of my wonderful partner, my beloved body.

Please help me have compassion and mercy upon this precious gift – my physical form.

I bless, accept and unconditionally love my (arms, legs, stomach, weight - body areas) and/or (kidneys, heart, blood pressure – organs and systems).

I am so grateful to be alive. I could not be in physical without you! And because of your dedicated service, I can see a sunset, I can smell a newborn baby, I can love joyfully and unconditionally, I can fight for freedom, justice and compassionate action.

Thank you, thank you thank you my Beloved Body, Bio-Mesh!

Prayer of Intent for Relationships

Jesus, Mary and the Magdala, The Tower of Strength please bless me with your Presence.

Angels and Archangels, especially calling upon Archangel Raphael for healing and empowerment, Archangel Gabriel for broadcasting and receiving the communications of love, and Archangel Chamuel who works with the Beloved and Soul Mates... please hear my plea!

In the Ocean of Love an Connection, I seek respectful love and connection!

In the Ocean of Intimacy and Partnership, I seek appropriate intimacy and partnership

In the name of the Beloved, I seek to love and be loved, to embrace and be embraced, to cherish and be cherished, to adore and be adored.

I ask this in Jesus's Name.

Serami Amor, Serami Ador, I ask this in the Sacred Heart Energies.

Blessings and Thank You!

Prayer of Intent for Abundance

In this Universe of Lavish, Infinite, Abundance

I claim my birthright as a Child of God,

> *as a Christed Light*

> *as a Co-Creator Energy of Consciousness*

Abundance is my birthright!

Unconditional love and support is my heritage!

Connection and awareness of Higher Consciousness is my

destiny. It is Who I Truly Am.

I step forward in my I AM Lineage to claim swim and play in the ocean of abundance.

May we All Ascend into this Knowingness!

There is enough for All!

There is more than enough for All!

We are all One.

So Be It!

Prayer of Intent to Begin Your Healing Practice

I call upon the highest forces of Love Light and Healing energies

I call upon those Beings who work with me and who work within the light grid of this bejeweled and blessed planet

I call upon Archangel Raphael to be with me as I step forward and offer my healing work to others

I call upon my Soul, my Highest and Greatest Self, and my direct I AM Lineage to be present

I call upon the Healing Masters, Healing Angels, and Healing Guides to align with me as I step forward as I step forward with my healing service

   (take a step forward)

I now breathe life into (name of your business) and set the intent to encourage it to blossom into fullness,

I send a golden invitation to those who can benefit from this work.

Thank you for this opportunity! I am so grateful to walk this destiny path of Healer

I am humble in the face of Infinity!

Prayer of Intent to Increase Your Healing Practice

Please allow my gifts of dedicated service and healing intent to send a broadcast throughout the world to those who would benefit from working with me in (name of business).

Mudra: Put hands around mouth like a bullhorn and allow your vibrations to emanate from you in concentric circles outward

Mudra: Cone of Power. Envision or draw a concentric circle starting tighter at your root chakra and expanding outward above your head.

I intend that those who can benefit from working with me hear my broadcast. I send a clarion call as a Lightworker.

Thank you for this opportunity to serve!

Prayer of Intent for Help with Animal Companions

Creator Essence, the Mother Father God, Creative Spark

Angels, Archangels and Healing Masters.

Overlighting Canine Angels (or Feline Angels, Equine Angels, etc.) please be with me and with (name of animal).

Bring your healing graces to my beloved companion so that she can feel her way back to wholeness and healing energies once again.

If there is anything that I should know for (Pet's) healing, please bring this information to me easily and effortlessly.

Thank you for the opportunity to bond with this magnificent Being of Love and Light and for the opportunity to do this work!

I send healing and comforting energies to all companion animals, especially (dogs, cats, etc.) who are in need: to those who are abandoned, lost, captured in labs, and in all manner of harsh environments.

Let there be healing and understandings of the joys of working with our companion species. Let there be love, justice, compassionate action and playful associations with these Beloveds.

Amen.

Prayer of Intent for Global Issues

In the Mandala of Wholeness, I step forward and step through dimensions of time and space to dance this dream awake, especially those who work with (name the situation).

(Then broaden or define it.)

Ascended Light Masters – You who align with the Light Grid of Gaia, hold the web of Lightworkers, and the increase of light and hope upon this blessed planet

Yogic masters – You who beam throughout time space and dimension, please be with me as I open my heart center to align with the Heart of the Divine. I open to the Sacred Heart Energies and those Beings who beam compassion and tolerance upon the Earth.

I expand my mind and will to align with Divine Intent and the evolution of consciousness at this time.

May my unique voice and expression shine forth in a clarion call in this time of blossoming and shift of the Light Quotient.

Namaste.

Rosary Renew

For those who enjoy the ritual of saying the Rosary, here is a renewed version of the three basic prayers which I have been guided to offer you as traditional Prayers of Intent.

Hail Mary

Hail, Mary! Full of grace
The Lord is with thee and me

Blessed art thou among women and men
And Blessed is the fruit of thy womb

Jesus
Jesua ben Josef
The Christed Light Within

Holy Mary
Mothering God!

Be with us always
now --
and with every in and out breath

Amen

Glory Be

Glory be to the Creator Source Energy

the Ever-Infinite Expanse
the Ever-Nurturing Love
and
the Ever-Creative Grace

As it was in the beginning
is now
and ever shall be

Whirls within whorls
within worlds

Amen

Our Grace

Our Mothering, Fathering,
Creator Source
Who art in all things

Hallowed be the Holy Name

Our time is come
Our Co-Creator will is done
Throughout all time, space
and dimension

Gift us this day
our daily breath

Forgiveness, kindness and compassion
we embrace for
ourselves
and for all others

Let us be conscious
of our Divinity
with every breath we take

Amen

Vocal Harmonics

Songs for Middle of Healing Sessions

Within Your Eyes

Opening

Overlighting Angels

Instant Replay

The Right Time

Land of a Dreamer

Melody

Within Your Eyes
(Ode to our Inner Child)

I see
Within me
My ability
My charity
My security
My serenity
My purity
My destiny

I love you, Child
Sweet inner child
With your trusting smile
And your freestyle
You make me worthwhile

You are best friend to me
You believe in me
You trust in me
You know the real me
Listening, always listening

You work hard just for me
You bear loads just for me
You hide secrets and shames just for me
Working, always working

Come to me now
I soothe your brow
I'm asking you how

Can I forget you
Or neglect you
My Inner child?

Still, you are unbowed
And always devoted to me now
And now,
and now,
and now

I love you Child
My inner child
With your trusting smile
And your freestyle
You make me worthwhile

I see
Within me
My ability
My charity
My security
My serenity
My purity
My destiny

(Mudra for Inner Child Healing)
Self -love
Self -acceptance
Self -forgiveness
Self -fulfillment

(Note for mudra in last paragraph: Fold your hands over each other at your heart center. For each affirmation, ex. Self-love, allow hands to open and pour self-love into the client's field for their Inner Child healing.)

Opening

Open my root
(motion 1st Root chakra)

Open my womb
(motion 2nd Sacral chakra)

Open my will
(motion 3rd Solar Plexus chakra)

Open my heart
(motion 4th Heart chakra)

Open my voice
(motion 5th Throat chakra)

Open my mind
(motion 6th Brow chakra)

Open my connection
(motion 7th Crown chakra)

Open my Lightbody
(motion 8th chakra above head - Transpersonal chakra)

Open my Incarnation
(motion 9th chakra below feet - Earth star chakra)

Open my Soul contracts
(motion 10th chakra above head – Soul Star chakra)

Open my Quantum DNA
(motion 11th chakra outside body – Multidimensional chakra)

Open my I AM Presence
(motion 11th chakra above body – OM consciousness)

Overlighting Angels

Gaia, Gaia, Gaia, Gaia

We have a voice
We sound our tone
We sing of joy
For our Gaia home

Open to our tome
Come home, come home

We swim we leap
We dive we deep
We soar we sweep
We walk concrete
We lay at your feet
In sacrificial heap
We are Gaia's Keep!

We buzz we creep
We clack we peep
We silently weep
Our messages seek
Our covenants keep
We are Gaia's Sweep!

Open to our tome
Come home, come home

We bring love and devotion
Mystery in motion
Freedom commotion

Opening Quantum Doorways

(you call us dog, cat, horse)

We soar in delight
Iridescent flight
Coloring your life
(you call us insect, bird)

We sound watery lore
From time immemore
Our purpose galore
(you call us whale, dolphin, fish)

We walk upon land
Bring adventures at hand
We are the ancient trans-
Formers morph from sea to land
(you call us mammal, reptile, amphibian)

We sound truth as we bark, croak and bray
Hear us say! Hear us say!
We share this home today!
Our together time you fray!
Hear our calls today
For our together stay

Side by side, thru the tides of time
This is our Home! Our Gaia Home!
Come home, come home!

(Note: This song is appropriate for those who intend to work with our animal companions or for those who need additional grounded connection to Gaia.)

Instant Replay

There's an Instant Replay every day
Sudden Grace
Clears out a space

With another try
I land sublime
Obstacles that blocked my way
Move away
Cannot stay today
It makes me wanna fly
Open my heart wide
Rise above the sky
Open my wings high

It's a foreground, background
Journey to the inside
Miracles unfolding
one more time

Catch a shooting star
With Guides and Loved Ones
Always there
Helping us align

Because I really want to fly
And I never need to wonder why

We are more than separate souls
On separate by-ways
There's one mountain top
That we need to climb

There's an Instant Replay

Opening Quantum Doorways

Every day
Sudden Grace
We are embraced!
It makes me wanna fly
Open my heart wide
Rise above the sky
Open my wings high

Music and lyrics by Tony Cardo

The Right Time

There's a time for moving forward
And a time for standing still
There's a time for elevation
And a time to push your will

But with all the contemplation
And a life that moves so fast
I need to be here with You
We're gonna make it last

And like the daylight
comes each morning
Bringing hope
A brand- new day
It's a life of celebration
There is no other way

This is the moment, when we show it
There is a hunger, and we know it

This is the right time
This is the right time
This is the right time

For us all!

Music and lyrics by Tony Cardo

Land of a Dreamer

I've seen you before
I'll see you again
My Precious Love

Your silent song
Reached me again today

Flag of love, flag of my heart
Raised in joy, Raised in wisdom
It's a land where only simple hearts can play

Hear the calling tonight taking the clouds away
In the land of a dreamer, Dreams come true today

And my piece of the sky
I have to reach for it
Nothing comes easy they say
I have to fly
Come my emotion
Soul has a witness Today!

Break out! Never leave a doubt
Straight to the top, Right from the heart

Break Out! Never leave a doubt
Stand while the world keeps turning around

I've seen you before
I'll see you again,
My Precious Love

Your silent song
Reaches to me today

Song and lyrics by Tony Cardo

Melody

Melody
I can feel you coming near to me
And the sunshine that you bring to me each time
It makes me want to cry

Melody
There is music coming from your heart
You are ever bringing me apart from pain
I want to live again within your love

And I know how lovely life can be
And if I call your Name,
Will you come and rescue me?
And, if you want me to,
I'll bring the world to you
If you'll just let me
sing Your Song

Melody
With the brightness of the morning sun
Bring the sunshine to the only one
I see
The one I want to be

Melody
With the treasure of your shining grace
With a whisper
And without a trace of time
All there is of mine I give to you

All there is of mine
I give to you

All therc is of mine
I give to you

Music and lyrics by Tony Cardo

Part 4

Guided

Visualizations

Chapter 8

Step One: The Portal
Visualizations that are Guided

Imagination is a creative marvel. Guided Visualizations can move us beyond this threshold of creative imagination into multidimensional space.

Telepathy is defined as thought transference.

Guided Visualizations can be described as stepping beyond time, space, and dimension in a Guided sense. This is temporal transference, spatial transference and, well, multidimensionality or working in the quantum. We do this naturally in dream states. Now, we are doing it consciously.

There are many people who present wonderful visualizations on www.Youtube.com, podcasts, and websites. There are three basic types of visualizations:

1. Some are imaginative, playful and creative.

2. Some are peaceful, meditative and soothing.

3. Some are, truly, portals into multidimensional space, and are Guided, or channeled by a higher energy.

Each of these three types of visualizations (imaginative, meditative, and Guided) are worthwhile. Each has power and purpose for us and for our clients. Healers make use of all three types of visualizations.

As a young student of psychology and counseling in the 60's and 70's, we were taught that only 'behaviorism' was a relevant and appropriate therapy and model for therapy. This meant that only actions and behaviors were worthy of our focus. This applied for both humans and animals, through environmental stimulus, in a conditioning pattern. Thoughts, emotions, or inner understandings had no impact on behavior or in our lofty psychological regard. Strange, indeed! But this was the thrust of psychology from the late 1800's through the 1980's when computerized models came into vogue.

At that time, I was very surprised to be taught in school a visualization known as 'systematic desensitization'. This was guided – not Guided! The therapist led us on a detailed tour of our body, from the tips of our toes to the tops of our heads. We were told, body part by body part, to tense our muscles, hold the tension, then release and move to the next part of our body. We were told this was acceptable in psychological worldview and got the seal of approval from behaviorists.

At the same time in my training, I was attending a Catholic, prayer-based college, was learning an esoteric system of meditation, (internally guided), and was leading myself out of labyrinths of family pain, but none of these inner experiences were accepted by the psychology power base as 'real'. Only behaviorism and systematic desensitization.

Now, we live in a world awash with examples of visualizations – auditory, visual, kinesthetic. We are free to roam (inside ourselves) without being judged (too much). Meditation, mindfulness and consciousness are on the rise!

Feel free to learn about the visualizations that are imaginative, playful and creative. Feel free to learn visualizations that are peaceful, meditative and soothing. 'Swim with dolphins', 'sleep in a rainforest', 'float with bubbles over the horizon', 'enter the cells of your body and bring light to every organ and system'. There are so many wonderful examples of the first two types of creative and meditative visualizations!

For our purposes, as Lightworkers, we have access to the 3rd, Guided, type of visualization. This is what we will be covering in Opening Quantum Doorways.

In order to step into the quantum or into multidimensionality, I recommend that you review the first part of this book, Standing at the Brink of Infinity. There are also many wonderful books on quantum healing techniques and the science behind our intuitive and transcendent work. I have listed many of them in the reference section for you.

They range from a number of books that could be titled, 'Quantum for Dummies' to more rigorous one replete with scientific jargon and squiggly line formulas. Don't be intimidated! It's very powerful (for us non-mathematical folk) to say, "Oh, I'm currently reading a book on quantum theory and applications." Eyebrows will raise! Of course, our 'theory and applications' entail the underpinings of energy healing – something quantum physicists squirm and scorn over.

Reading, or skimming, through this information helps in multiple ways. We need to have a foundation to replace the one that has been put into our brains since our first breath on this planet. As detailed in Part 1, our entire society has been churning between strong worldviews – religious and scientific. Both have a kernel of 'truth' imbedded, but both are woefully lacking.

Jean Piaget, a genius of cognitive developmental education, detailed the process of young children and their understanding of the world. The four stages are:

- Sensorimotor stage: birth to 2 years
- Preoperational stage: ages 2 to 7
- Concrete operational stage: ages 7 to 11
- Formal operational stage: ages 12 and up

To move from one stage to another, children are very active. They perform 'experiments' (much like my laying on the bed, closing one eye at a time) and thereby learn about how the world works. Interestingly, Piaget theorized that children do not add continually to their permanent knowledge base, like a child who continues to add blocks to make a tower. Instead, when new information or ways of viewing the world become apparent, the old knowledge base (tower) crumbles and a new configuration is built, immediately, from scratch. Interesting theory!

Do you remember how you learned about the world and how/why it works the way it does from birth to age 2? Probably you hold no memories of that time, as much of your experience was non-verbal and not able to be filed and retrieved. You might have some scenes imbedded from 2 – 7 years of age, perhaps memories of important people or details. Remember how you learned and viewed the world from ages 7 – 11 years of age? 12 years old? All of this cognitive mind mapping is done before we even reach high school!

As Lightworkers, working within the quantum with Guided Visualizations, we are similar to children moving from stage to stage. Perhaps, it would be more honest to say that we could consider adding a 5th stage of cognitive development, which would include moving from being a guileless observer and reactor to a leading- edge co-creator, one who is opened to higher vibrational frequencies, both from within and from telepathic communications. It might take a while for cognitive developmental researchers and educators to acknowledge this step.

Guided Visualizations are very powerful tools in energy healing and in personal connection and empowerment! How to do this? Let's start!

Grounding, Safe and Secure

Crossing boundaries from 3D (consensual reality) into multidimensional inner landscapes is possible and real. Within the quantum. What is more real than the basis of reality?

Paradoxically, as Beings enmeshed in our partner, our body, and rooted to another partner, our Earth, we are able to go the furthest afield when we are grounded the most. It sounds counterintuitive but, consider tall trees. Those that grow high into the sky are very rooted into the Earth and are stable for hundreds, even thousands of years. Trees that have shallow roots are easily uplifted in a storm. In our fractal, or repeating patterned universe, the same holds true for us. To go high, root deep.

If you don't look up to the sky (possibilities), you run the risk of a hidebound life. If you don't ground yourself deeply, you run the risk of being spacey, unable to manifest those things you want the most. It is a delicate dance to root and reach – just the right amount. Ground into and appreciate your 3D perspectives and skills – and then open the doors to multidimensionality. Opening doorways in the quantum can be accomplished through Guided Visualizations as well as Prayers of Intent.

As Spirit-Made-Flesh, enveloped in our bio-mesh, we humans like to feel safe, secure, and grounded to our Gaia partner.

Breath work is a common way to have the client relax and deepen into their bodies and into the Earth. It is my chosen way to do this. I start a session by encouraging the client to take three breaths and I talk them through both the inbreath and outbreath. Three seems a good suggestion – not too vague ("breathe") or too detailed ("breathe in and count to 4, hold for 4, breathe out for 4, hold for 4"). Three feels like the Goldilock zone for me.

I also encourage clients to relax and creatively visualize roots growing from the soles of their feet into the Earth, so they feel safe, secure, and grounded. See the Conscious Human Tree, below, for my go-to grounding visualization.

Another subtle message is to say "Visualize" instead of "Imagine". In a light trance state, you are putting forth suggestions. There are coded subtexts for these words. 'Visualize' is a stronger word, more rooted to our senses. It also implies actively looking within, a precursor to clairvoyance. 'Imagine' commonly means it is not real; it's child's play, ephemeral. We are making all this up. My experience of decades of doing this work is that it absolutely is not illusory. It is quite real and working in the quantum in this way helps move stuck energies faster than therapeutic talking models.

To meet the client where they exist, on the 3D level, you might choose a body- oriented visualization. You then begin to step the client into a deeper state to make the crossing, if they choose. You might even go back to the example of 'systematic desensitization', encouraging them to relax muscles from their toes to their head.

Client Choice

I offer a choice for those who have their own personal methods to go within or who feel anxious about following another person's suggestion. This is perfectly reasonable to me and I don't judge if they refuse my overtures.

Their anxiety could be for a number of reasons – they could not like to be directed to an inner space. More commonly, they don't understand what 'visualizing' means and judge themselves as not being able to do it.

The imagery, also, could be confronting or against their personal belief system – so be circumspect and discerning when using Guided Visualizations. Know your client well or choose a very safe, familiar doorway. Nature-based ones are almost always acceptable, especially short groundings into the earth and openings from the crown chakra.

I often start the sessions by saying,

> *"I will start with a Prayer of Intent – is that OK with you? Next, I'll offer you a Guided Visualization. You can follow my suggestions, or instead, find a safe place you know, maybe even a place you have visited. Visualize that scene and enjoy spending time there."*

"Sometimes, people fall asleep during the visualization and session. It's perfectly fine to fall asleep – sometimes healings go deeper when we're asleep."

"You could also stay awake and ask questions that come up and I will do my best to get answers for you. Highest and greatest good for all."

Following are two versions of my basic Grounding Visualization, The Conscious Human Tree.

Grounding with the Conscious Human Tree

The following Guided Visualization, either in its entirety or a shortened version (version 1 or 2), is one I use with almost every client session. I might even silently place the imagery on the client by following my hands down their body, down their feet into the earth, and opening up their crown chakra, motioning to the heavens if, for whatever reason, I don't want to speak the visualization.

By starting a session with the Conscious Human Tree, you ground yourself and your client; you affirm for them that they are safe and secure, and in sacred space. I state a Prayer of Intent either before or after the Conscious Human Tree and then follow with a healing session, many times following the Grounding with opening the portal and stepping through.

Grounding is the first step so that you feel tethered enough to trust and skip through the quantum doorway.

Where you go afterwards is … well, anywhere and anywhen!

Grounding: Conscious Human Tree (1)

"Let's begin by taking 3 conscious breaths together. It feels so good to breathe in. We are filled up easily, effortlessly, completely. We don't need to gulp down or bring in more air than we need. Just the right amount comes in. We don't need to force or push more air out of our lungs. When we breathe out, just the right amount goes out. Like a wave. We relax and feel safe in this embrace, in this swing of our breath"

"Follow your next breath down your body, down your torso, down your legs, and out the soles of your feet. Follow your breath down as if they are roots, going as far deep into the Earth that feels comfortable for you. Past the foundation layers, the soil and water table levels. Anchor in where you feel safe."

"Now breathe up from your roots, from the Earth. Bring the beautiful colors of the Earth up through your feet, up your legs, up your torso, up and out the top of your head like a cascading waterfall of liquid light. Breathe as Earth colors wash through you. Breathe in the green of the grass, the blue of the sky, the lavender and pink and peach of the sun- set. Breathe in gold, silver, purple, yellow, orange, all the beautiful Earth colors, which bathe us in their colors, bringing us rejuvenation, balance, healing, and joy."

"With your next breath open the top of your head, your crown chakra. Visualize yourself like a tree, with your trunk, branches and leaves going up, up, up. They ascend upwards and open their canopy right outside the Earth's atmosphere, in the heavens, opening up like an umbrella."

"Breathe in swirling solar colors, the iridescent and pearlescent pastel colors of the solar storms. Breathe them down through your branches, down through your head, down your torso, down your roots and into the Earth. The colors are coded by our Solar Angel and enter the Earth's magnetics where they are coded and decoded through you, through your DNA, bringing your unique tone into the Earth."

"Breathe again from the earth, from your roots, coding through your DNA, up again into the heavens, sounding your unique I AM tone."

"And here we stand as Conscious Trees.
Spanning heaven and earth.
Finite and infinite.
Mortality and immortality."

This is the full Guided Visualization for the Conscious Human Tree.

You can try this complete version, or simply give the suggestion and encouragement to a shorter version.

Conscious Human Tree (2)

"Take 3 conscious breaths, enjoying the feeling of following your breath down your body, into your legs and feet and then, like roots, into the earth."

"The next breath, breathe up from your feet, your roots bringing the beautiful earth colors up from your legs, your body, your arms and out your head in a cascading rainbow of liquid light. Bring green, and gold, and blue, and violet, pink, and orange and all the beautiful colors."

"On your next breath, open your crown chakra and visualize a tree growing from you up into the heavens. Breathe down the pearlescent and iridescent colors of the heavens down into your head, your body, and the earth. Mixing with the earth colors, you feel the swirling colors that you really are."

"And, here we are,

Conscious Human Trees,

spanning heaven and earth,

finite and infinite,

mortality and immortality."

Conscious Human Tree spanning heaven and earth.

Image by Mariana Ruzsak Hollo.

Opening and Crossing the Portal

After your Prayer of Intent and a Grounding suggestion, the next step, literally is to create/find and walk through a portal or doorway. Stepping beyond it will take you from 3D to multi-D space. We wish to expand and elevate to sacred space where healing takes place. For the client these portal visualizations serve as doorways to and through the quantum or what is possible, what is real.

Like the board game *Clue*, we can, with the right throw of the dice, shift from one location to another, one dimensional space to another. In *Clue*, we find secret passageways from the Kitchen to the Study, and from the Lounge to the Conservatory. Four secret passageways (portals) in the 3D mansion.

In our energy sessions with clients, just as in Clue, multidimensionality is a breath away, a thought away (or a dice away). As we breathe and think within 3D structures, it helps to set a framework to cross. A doorway or portal is an easy way to go. We normally cross a doorway to change venues. Here, we are crossing dimensions and opening the veil between worlds by crossing a threshold in our mind, with an intent and our right to do so.

The following are some wonderful doorways I have traversed. Some are my favorites... try them and discover yours!

Archway of Flowers

An archway of flowers is my number 1 favorite dimensional portal. I start with a visual suggestion:

> *"Walk through a meadow scene on a beautiful day. See yourself walking on a path of rainbow colored small stones.*

> *"Up ahead is an archway of flowers. We are excited to cross under the arch because we know an adventure is at hand. As we step underneath the archway, we can smell beautiful flowers and scent of roses and jasmine, lilacs and honeysuckle… the scent is so inviting!"*

> *"As we pass under the arch, the scene is the same – and yet it's not. The sky appears bluer, the grass greener, the birdsong sweeter and clearer."*

> *"We can hear the trickle of water flowing off and to the right. We follow the path through some trees and find a beautiful scene! There is a gentle waterfall flowing into a small pond. It is so peaceful and serene here."*

You may have walked under an archway of flowers on one of your travels, both in nature and in dreams or visions. Adding a flower is a plus. The color and shape of the flower is implied. The scent increases our clairalience, or clear smelling. It is one of the gift orders, not commonly mentioned. Interestingly, many Saintly apparitions occur with roses (Mary and St. Theresa as major ones). Bring your own garden suggestions forward and incorporate them into your portals.

Waterfall

There are so many wonderful examples of waterfalls – large and small. In my favorite visualization, the Archway of Flowers, we move next to the Waterfall, which I call The Sacred Grove.

> *"You become aware of a sweet sound of water falling. You follow the sound to the right, through a small thicket of trees. You follow a dirt path and come upon a beautiful scene. There is a small waterfall flowing into a little pond. It feels so safe and secure here."*

> *"You can sit by the edge of the pool, dive within the water, lay on the stones that are on the banks. You can also choose to walk behind the waterfall. The water looks rainbow colored in the sunlight. As you step behind the waterfall, you realize there is a small opening. You step inside…"*

Ancient Tree

A tree is another known place for a multidimensional portal.

> *"Visualize walking on a summery day through a sweet- smelling forest. Up ahead is a large tree with sheltering boughs. You are drawn to the tree and are excited to rest your back against its comforting presence."*

> *"The Tree feels nurturing, like a mother's embrace. It almost feels alive and senses you there. You are so welcomed! You watch squirrels play up and down the truck and branches and hear birds calling to each other. You feel safe and secure."*

> *"As you sit against the trunk, you feel a round knob behind you. As you turn to look, you realize that there is a door in the tree trunk! The knob has engravings and feels like it was smoothed by many loving hands over hundreds or thousands of years. You turn the knob, the door swings inward and you step within…"*

Bridge

Bridges take us from one territory to another and so they are perfect for our portal. Many people understand that, by crossing a bridge, they are moving from one location to another. It is a natural portal, even in 3D. Here, we are looking to step between dimensions as well.

"See yourself walking up to a bridge that signifies where you are now in your life. Visualize, clearly, this bridge. It can be a rope bridge, a wooden bridge, or even a steel bridge. It could also be a glass bottom bridge or a covered bridge. It could even be an invisible bridge. See your bridge now."

"Look around you. Where are you? Are you in the mountains, crossing a large canyon? Or, perhaps you are at the sea shore, spanning a body of water below you. Perhaps you are in trees, crossing a forest canopy. Your bridge is strong! It has stood for many, many years and will continue to stand for many more. Look and feel your way to your bridge."

"As you cross the bridge, you feel safe and excited, and you know there is an adventure at hand. You are crossing over to somewhere special."

"Half way across the bridge, you notice a cloud fogs your vision of the path across. You can see your feet and you can see your immediate surroundings. But, it seems like you are now walking, safely, in the clouds.

In a breath, the clouds part, and you see you are entering a new land..."

Mountain Cave

You might feel comfortable in the mountains. We use parallels of scaling a mountain for achieving heights of higher awareness and conquering personal challenges. You could design a visualization walking up the mountain, or getting to a plateau, overlooking a far- ranging vista. Another possible portal is in a cave.

> *"See yourself effortlessly climbing a short mountain path as it crosses around boulders and bushes. It is a bright day and you feel energized, safe, and excited as you walk this path. You pass small creeks to the side of you and see small blueberry bushes which you can stop and refresh yourself with. You know this mountain well. You have been here before many times. In dreams you have visited. In airplanes you may have crossed it. In real life you may know of a special mountain that calls your name."*

> *"You come to a fork in the path. You know you can't choose a wrong path – they all lead up! You choose your favorite path and follow its winding step. Up ahead, you see an interesting shape in the mountainside. You know what this is! There is a large, oval opening, which leads you directly into sacred space. You take a breath, bow your head, and enter within…"*

Crystal Doorway

A Crystal Doorway is a wonderful portal. It can lead you to a number of interesting places. Most healers and energy workers love to work with crystals and adorn themselves and their healing space with one or more favorites. I opened this crystal doorway during a Reiki attunement and it led to a chamber beyond.

"See yourself walking along a hilly landscape that you know and love. The path leads upwards, but there are many spaces to stop, rest, and refresh yourself. You have favorite vistas where you can sit and look out over a beautiful terrain. You can see far into the distance, almost to the horizon. The sun is still in the sky and it is such a beautiful day to make this ascent."

"Up ahead on the path you catch a glint of sunlight sparkling and shimmering. Where can the sunlight be striking on the mountain path? You follow the curve around the bend and ahead is an oval shape almost 8 feet high enclosed in the mountainside. The oval is made of crystal. It's a crystal doorway! You stand before this sublime space, feeling the pulsing energy coming from the crystal. Run your hands over the smooth crystal shape. Feel the outline of the doorframe, the doorknob, and take a peek through the round clear opening. As you stand there, mesmerized at the beauty you have found, you wonder how you can open the door and what possibly could be on the other side? With just the thought, your hand goes through the crystal, into the space beyond. Delighted, you follow…"

Sacred Shrine

Visiting a shrine not only offers a portal for crossing into multidimensional space, but it also has the advantage of allowing you an easy way to meet a known and Beloved Being of Love and Light who comes just for you.

Consider a sacred area you have visited. In Portland, Oregon, there is a magnificent Catholic site, called The Grotto which has an altar built into a large rock cliff. There are many shrines situated in mossy hills. There is even an elevator which runs up the cliffside to a second terraced area filled with more shrines and sacred spaces.

Or, perhaps Stonehenge or other megalithic structures call to you? These are effective and enticing portals as well. Follow your interest and, if possible, walk the land you wish to use as a portal.

> *"You walk along a well- worn path to a sacred grove, to a shrine of St. Francis, a saint you dearly love. You are bringing a colorful bouquet of flowers to place there. It's an edible offering and will be left as a gift for the wildlife in the area too."*

> *"As you are stand there, the statue begins to vibrate. It elongates into 6 feet high and you can see a shaft of light peering through. As you look you see St. Francis step up and out of the shrine and come forward to meet you!"*

> *"He motions to a nearby bench for the both of you to sit on. It feels so relaxing and safe to be in the presence of such a gentle and loving soul. You hear and understand each other without even speaking any words. Spend time with this Light Being Who loves and cherishes you and your work."*

Bubble Membrane

This portal emerged during an advanced energy training attunement class. I frequently use the Archway and Waterfall portals to enter the Healing Hall and the Hall of Healing Masters. When I began to intone this imagery, a Bubble Membrane appeared behind the waterfall and it led directly into a Quantum DNA Activation Chamber. I was surprised but delighted!

> *"We are walking through a meadow of flowers on a bright and beautiful day. Up ahead is an Archway of Flowers. We have been here before. We know this is a portal to sacred space. As we cross under, we hear the beautiful waterfall up ahead. It is so peaceful here, at the waterfall. We decide to take a moment to breathe in the scent of the woods and the flowers."*

> *"We walk along the pond, to the back of the waterfall. Right behind the waterfall, there is a shimmering, iridescent bubble right in the rock wall! At first, we might think it's a trick of the sunlight, like a prism passing through the waterfall. But then we press our hands onto the rock wall. It feels rough and cool. We put our hands through the spray of the gentle waterfall. It feels delightful, like liquid light."*

> *Feeling safe and enchanted, we put our hands on the iridescent Bubble which has stretched now to 8 feet wide and high. Our hand goes right through! We smile and step through."*

> *"We enter straight into a chamber that is covered in crystals…"*

Watery Portals

This category contains the elements of going deep within a watery portal. We can be submerged or swimming in more shallow waters. Going underwater is a dimensional shift even in our 3D realm. It can be wonderfully peaceful and serene for some – but could also be frightening to those who have a fear of water. Know your client well before using this imagery.

> *"It is a wonderfully warm day and you are at a secluded beach. You have the sun and sand and gentle waves all to yourself. You can see there are people swimming and children playing in the water about ½ mile down. But your area is more private. It's just for you."*

> *"Feel the wind in your hair and smell the salt water tang on your tongue. It's a delicious day! You step into the water and feel the cool and refreshing temperature. You love the way you feel in the water as the waves seem to caress you. A deep fluid sound comes from within you. Hmmmmmmm. This song of your heart echoes in the watery depths. You hear an answering song."*

> *"You are being invited to swim deeper into a fluid, multidimensional space. You answer 'yes' to the invitation! Whales and dolphins are coming in answer to your song."*

> *"You are able to breathe naturally as you play with these companions. Up ahead is a vortex opening. With anticipation and joy, you swim into the opening…"*

Dancing in the Clouds

As with water, flying in the air is a complementary way of leaving our earth's gravity and entering another realm. With water, we go deep. With air, we fly high.

"As you take a walk along a beautiful plateau, see colorful wildflowers and hear sounds of stillness. You have visited here before, maybe in dreams? It is the perfect place to practice flying!"

"Walk to the edge of the plateau and look at the orange hued canyons surrounding this sacred land. Flex your shoulders and release your wings as you peer upwards at the birds gliding around your head, encouraging you to flap your wings and soar."

"There are Angels and so many beautiful birds encouraging you to allow the air drafts lift you easily from earth's gravity. Open your wings and soar, dancing with the playful currents."

"Enjoy this soaring, gliding, riding time in the sky with feather and angelic friends. Take as long as you like here in the sky. When you're ready for the next adventure, look over your shoulder into the cloud bank that has arisen on your right."

"As you fly closer, you can begin to make out another world, a familiar, healing and learning space. Fly through!"

Spiral Staircase

Moving from our nature theme, there are also portals that can be accessed from a number of venues. A spiral staircase is a strong portal and has been used by hypnotherapists for many years. We are not intending to hypnotize or regress clients. We are intending to allow them to relax, go deeper, and, if they choose, step into a Guided state for deep healing and empowerment to occur.

"Ahead of you is a beautiful spiral staircase. The stairs are made of white marble, with a thread of gold running throughout the marble. The railing is embellished with carved scrolling designs. It feels soft to your hand and it is so inviting to touch. Almost like an old friend."

"The staircase winds upward from your platform. As you peer above, you see there are colorful stained windows running the length of the staircase. There are designs which take your breath away, they are so beautiful and inviting. What are the images? Who can the pictures represent?"

"Look closely as you begin to walk up the stairs. You have entered on level 3. Climb the staircase to level 4, level 5, level 6."

"With energy to spare, you reach your destination, level 7. You and the door are bathed in the colors of the stained- glass window to your left. There are golden and violet and pink iridescent colors bathing you as you open the door. The handle is made of pearl. Open and step within…"

Elevator

Much like the spiral staircase, you can easily move through multidimensional space within an elevator. You can enter at any numbered level you choose and exit at any level. Basic knowledge of numerology is always fun to include. As with the staircase, you can choose to go up or go down. Either takes you here, there, and everywhere.

"Up ahead of you there is a gleaming elevator which you know you have ridden before. This elevator takes you to many places within the realm of the sacred."

"You walk to the gleaming white platform and notice the floor you are on is number 11, a number denoting Mastery. This is where you're getting on! Exciting to think where you're getting off!"

"The elevator door opens, and you walk into a small enclosed space. You hear lilting music playing. The lighting is an evanescent pink!"

"As you ascend, you notice that you are feeling happy and expectant of what will unfold. You have been in this elevator before, so you're not surprised when the elevator exits the building!"

"It takes you for a ride on the outside of the elevator shaft and you can see the scene before you. Dazzling lights from a cityscape. Dazzling starlights in the sky. Up the elevator keeps going. Across a rooftop garden you see a peaceful scene below you. You are almost there."

The door opens, and you step out onto the rooftop garden where you meet..."

Door 22

In a dream I saw myself in a carriage looking for a particular address. I looked out the window and saw my destination: '22' ornately posted on a very large, golden door. I met my Mother-in-Law and spoke at length with her.

As usual for these types of contacts, she looked younger than I knew her to be – maybe late 30's. She had brown hair, a shade I never saw on her. She also wore a long red robe, something I had never seen her in. After I awoke I described the dream to my husband; he said he saw his mother in a red robe many times when he was younger. It was her favorite color and her favorite robe.

Consider going yourself or taking a client to Door 22 when you are intending to contact a Loved One who has passed.

> *"Feeling safe and secure, see yourself traveling in a beautiful carriage, white and gold, horse drawn carriage, through streets of a town or city that seems familiar to you. There are Beings of Love and Light right next to you for comfort, safety and support. Your Guardian Angel is there with you. Archangel Michael is there with you."*

> *"You are looking for a particular address, number 22, and, as you look out the beautiful carved window frame of the carriage, you see a tall golden door engraved with the number '22'. You have arrived at your destination! The door is so beautiful, about 15 or 20 feet high. You stop the carriage and open the door."*

> *"Immediately inside you see a marble staircase going straight up. You ascend the stairs. At the top of the landing, you see a large room, filled with Beings of Love and Light, some who you have known in this lifetime. Some you dearly would love to see, hug, and talk to who have transitioned."*

> *"Coming to meet you is the person you most dearly wish to see and speak to! You see them clearly, although they look younger, lighter, perhaps happier than you remember them."*

"Spend some time with them now, asking your questions, telling them how much you love them and miss them. Be sure to listen to what they have to say to you!"

Apparating

For Harry Potter fans, apparating is a well -known means of teleporting from one location to another. In the Potterverse, you only need to fully focus on where you wish to appear, feel that experience through your body … and go. Perhaps this is what we do when we dream – we appear and disappear (or apparate and disapparate) according to another set of rules – not logic or conscious volition).

I have found that this method of using intent and focus easier going to realms, scenes, places, halls, etc. which we have already visited through dreamscape or Guided Visualizations. It is more challenging to will yourself through time, space and dimension without knowing where you are going!

> *"Take 3 deep breaths, root into the Earth, and open your crown chakra to the heavens. See yourself shimmering and filled with Light. As you vibrate higher and higher, you realize that you are expanding. The space within your atoms is infinite, your personal energy field, your energy signature, is connected to All There Is."*

> *"Take a breath and will yourself to the Sacred Grove. Move to the Hall of Healing Masters. Perhaps you would like to meet with others who have mastered the art of teleportation. Many have! If you wish, you can too."*

> *"Spend time with this wonderful skill you are perfecting. Where would you like to visit? Go there now."*

Cosmic Journeys

This portal is an interesting one for those who are more galactically-minded. The movie, *Contact,* showed one way to move between dimensions. I had a dream once, so vivid, that I climbed out of a hatch in a space ship and stood on the roof of the space ship, with my arms wide (like the iconic Titanic pose), hurtling through space. It was such an exhilarating dream, I still remember it 40 years later.

>*"We see ourselves hurtling through the stars in a cruising space ship. We are safe and secure in our cocooned hub of humanity, crossing interstellar space, time and dimension. This is our true home – the stars! We are stardust made conscious. We are home."*

>*"Look at the large wall console and see a magnificent view of the galaxy with its multicolored star systems. We can chart a course wherever we want!*

>*We turn a dial on the screen and see an iridescent vortex ahead. We know that we are in the right place, at the right time. We know this vortex well – it takes us from dimension to dimension in a blink of an eye. It tunnels a star strewn path through the star clusters and nebulae."*

>*"We set a course for the portal! We arrive…"*

Geometric Shapes

Some energy workers prefer not to work with Beings of Love and Light but align more fully with the sacredness of numbers and shapes, universal forms, fractals parsing into infinity.

Although any shape that calls to you is a great doorway, working with the Platonic solids, and Metatron's cube, are known avenues. You can order small versions of these esoteric objects online.

The Platonic Solids are 5 three dimensional shapes with equal sides and angles. They are:

- tetrahedron, 4 triangle faces

- cube, 6 square faces

- octahedron, 8 triangle faces

- dodecahedron, 12 pentagonal faces

- icosahedron, 20 triangle faces

Metatron's Cube is formed with 13 spheres interconnected with lines from the center of each sphere. This is known in energy circles as the Lightbody Merkaba. It contains all the 5 Platonic Solids and expands outward into the Flower of Life design – the template for creation.

The Merkaba is the rotating Lightbody field within Metatron's Cube. It is said that this shape actualizes our entire energetic field. Masters used this rotating form to materialize themselves and objects to and from dimensions. It is a fascinating part of esoteric knowledge.

"We are perfectly still within our breath. Move upwards to feel the vibrating oneness that envelopes us all. It shimmers within us and we can feel our field vibrate with this energy: in front of us, behind us, to the left of us, the right of us, above our heads and below our feet."

"Behold this shimmering as it continues to expand. This shimmering is us – our energy field! We expand our field to include the entire room: at least 10 feet to the front of us, to our back, to our left and right sides, above our heads and below our feet."

"We continue to expand and shimmer, our form becoming more light filled with each breath, each intent, each word. We begin to see our Merkaba – our Lightbody, shimmering with our lifeforce energies. We breathe and will our physical form within this shimmering templated form, this chariot of Light."

"In our Lightbody Merkaba we can go anywhere in the universe, faster than the speed of light! Let's explore!"

Go There Yourself Before, and During a Client Journey

As you can see, there are many portals to move between dimensions. Go there with your client. Don't just speak the words, follow the experience as well! This will allow you, as the Lightworker, to open the door and step through with your client, if they choose to follow.

In my experience, clients do like to follow the suggestions and often report wonderful experiences occurring while they are in this sacred space. Sometimes, this experience is more vivid and important to them than our hands-on healing. Don't underestimate the power of healings in this Guided journeying!

A good way to make this real for you is to visit the many types of portals and then work with ones that you enjoy. You are looking for safe and secure openings for yourself. If you feel inspired, safe and secure, your client will too. Quantum entanglement!

Consider places in nature or dreams that you have actually experienced. Walk in nature, go visit a waterfall, swim in a lake, walk over a bridge. Let these 3D, visceral experiences bring a sense of realism to your visualizations. You will then be able to more easily design visualizations from the first two categories – those that are creative and those that are peaceful.

The 3rd type of visualization, Guided, occurs through the alchemical pop, the Grace process, described in Books 1 and 2 of the *Tools for Lightworkers Series*. This alchemical pop of Grace envelopes us, as a gift from above. Allow Grace to enfold you, in possibility, in the quantum. Your intent and willingness to explore this infinite realm is the key. The two strands of Grace and intent interweave, as does our DNA, forming coherent and beautiful patterns.

Who is to say there really isn't a portal where you say there is?

That's the fascinating question.

If you walk through, can they follow?

My experience is, absolutely,

> Yes!

Design Your Unique Guided Visualization
Step 1: The Portal

    We're not in Kansas anymore. Play with a few portals you would like to cross.

Version 1:

Version 2:

Chapter 9

Step Two: The Journey

Opening the Portal, Step 1 in our Guided Visualizations, can be an end unto itself. You might wish for yourself as well as for a client, to stop after the opening, allowing for Grace and Spirit Guides to enter, dialogue with, and perhaps, even heal clients from that first multidimensional space. I allow my intuition to guide me in this process as to how far we journey.

For energy training classes, where clients are attuned to Reiki Healer practitioner and advanced levels, I offer one of the journeying experiences below. For clients who are having a healing session on the table, or as part of the Guided Counseling, immediate access is offered into one of these realms, especially the Hero's Journey and Inner Landscape.

Again, visit these (and other) places yourself. Enjoy the experience, look around, set markers for yourself, align it with your own personal 3D experiences so it is an easier 'jump' for you. And, then, begin to bring others along this journey. Here we act as Guide in the Realm of Multidimensionality and weave within the very structures of reality. Trust yourself if you feel excited about and guided to visit some of the more etheric 'places' below.

Sacred Grove

The Sacred Grove is one of my most favorite places to visit and to invite clients to. I have welcomed others to this space for decades, and it never gets old!

The Sacred Grove is a meeting place of Souls, Angels, Guides, Companion Animals and more. It is also a place of rest, rejuvenation, initiation, and purification.

I begin the journey there with the Archway of Flowers, described above and then segue into a beginning version of The Waterfall. From there, we open and step through…

> *"See yourself walking through a meadow scene on a beautiful day. It is the perfect temperature. You look down and see that you are walking on a path of rainbow colored small stones."*

> *"Up ahead is an Archway of Flowers. You are excited to cross under the arch into the Sacred Grove. As you step underneath the archway, you smell the inviting scent of roses and lilacs."*

> *"As you pass under the arch, the scene is the same – and yet it's not. The sky appears bluer, the grass greener, the birdsong sweeter and clearer. You can hear the trickle of water flowing off through some trees and follow a dirt path to a gentle waterfall. There is a small pond under the waterfall. It is so peaceful and serene here."*

> *"Sit for a while if you like or take off your shoes and step into the warm waters of the small pond, feeling refreshed and serene. You can dive within the water or lay on the stones that are on the banks. You know this Grove is safe and secure. Follow your heart's desires."*

"After a while, you notice that you are not alone!"

"Beings of Love and Light come visit you. Perhaps you see a Loved One who has crossed, or an Angel, or a Master. You might even notice that a beloved Companion Animal is there to greet you."

"They are here at the Sacred Grove which is a meeting place in Spirit. You are welcome and cherished! It is so wonderful to spend some time with these Beings who love you so dearly."

"Ask any questions you have, and listen for the answers..."

Hero's Journey

The Hero's Journey, based upon the work of Carl Jung and Joseph Campbell, touches upon the eternal in our life's details. I often use these Archetypes when working with a client.

The stages I use are:

1. Birth – magical or mysterious, each is unique

2. Youth – alienation, forming an identity

3. Finding a Mentor – feeling a call

4. The Quest – challenges, battles, obstacles

5. Death – ending of a job, relationship, health, etc.; there are so many deaths in our lifetime

6. The Underworld – wandering, lost, unsure

7. Rebirth – viscerally, a new life

8. Apotheosis – your legacy, your return with gift

Most clients come ... can you guess?

Clients come, commonly, during the Underworld stage when they feel lost and alone. In the 6th book of my Tools for Lightworkers Series, ARISE, A Soul Based Perspective on Counseling and Healing, we dedicate a chapter to Hero's Journey and Inner Landscapes found within the Journey, each unique to the client's path.

In Guided Visualizations, we often add this component into the journey to the Sacred Grove (above).

> *"You are here, at the Sacred Grove, a private meeting place with Spirit. You know you are known, welcomed, and cherished! It is so wonderful to spend some time with Light Beings who love you so dearly."*

> *"You notice that One, in particular, steps forward with a map. They unroll it on the ground in front of you as you both sit near the water-fall. You look and see - it's a map of your own personal Hero's Journey!"*

> *"You trace the path you have taken this lifetime, from birth on-wards. You see the quests and challenges you have faced throughout your contracted time. You have done so well! You have been in the right place at the right time, doing all the right things!"*

> *Now, you notice, exactly where you are at this moment in time. Feel free to discuss your Hero's Journey location with your Guide. There is always a higher perspective given to us by Spirit. Our choices, thoughts, words, deeds, are always viewed with compassion, kind-ness, and unconditional love. It is so reassuring to know that we have always done the best we could at every moment, in every challenge, including this one."*

> *"Take a little time, if you wish, to talk to this Being of Love and Light about your own Hero's Journey…"*

The Gifts

Often, Gifts come with the Hero's Journey, just before leaving the Grove. The Gifts come also during a class attunement, especially for Reiki 1 class and attunement.

I have often been amazed and brought to tears by a Gift I have been given as I talked a client through this passage. Once, I 'saw' John Lennon, a dearly beloved iconic figure for me. He 'gave' me a charcoal stub and I gave him a medal.

Intuitively, I knew that his gift to me, the charcoal, was his message to me to continue with my art, which is my writing. My medal to him was unusual. It reminded me that I don't have to be best at writing or publishing, or anything. I can give back the idea of external rewards. It was a very deep, personal, and moving experience for me – out of the 'blue'. Allow yourself to be surprised!

> *"You sit here, in the Sacred Grove, with your Guardian Angel, and spend some time going over your Personal Hero's Journey."*
>
> *"You realize your Guide has a Gift for you. This gift can be something to help you move forward with one of your challenges. Open your hands to receive the Gift now."*
>
> *"This Gift can be an object, a feeling, a quality, anything at all. Open and receive now."* (pause)
>
> *"And, you realize that you, too, have a Gift for them. You give them your Gift now. It can be a memory, or a prayer, a longing, an object, anything at all. Give Spirit your gift now."* (pause)
>
> *"If you are unsure of your Gift, know that you will become aware of it during your sleep tonight."*

This last part (if they are unaware of their gifts) I add, softly, to assuage those who get very tense, feeling that they didn't 'see' a gift or 'get' a gift. They can begin to doubt themselves, and the process.

A light suggestion helps your client relax and remain open to continuing with the gifting process during the next few hours, especially at night. I have not come across anyone who did not, eventually, receive a gift. And, it sometimes happens, that you will 'see' the gift for them. You might then decide to share your vision for them, or not. Check in with your Guidance first. However, I have seen their gift often. Such is the entangled field of the Quantum!

Inner Child: The Lake

The Lake is a well- known Inner Landscape destination in the Hero's Journey. I first encountered this space for myself and it was very informative and healing, although confronting. I 'saw' myself sitting at the edge of the Lake, with Loved Ones of mine in the water, calling for my help, swallowing water, thrashing about. I threw them life preservers, made them a makeshift raft, pointed out to them a boat was coming and encouraged them to climb on board. I held out a long branch and threw out a rope for them to grab onto.

They wouldn't take any of my efforts to save them. They wanted me in the water, drowning with them. It was so painful of an experience to watch them be in pain and fear, and to know that I couldn't help them. I could only drown myself, to prove my love and to be supportive of them and their choices. Finally, (it took many months of working this image) I decided I had to walk away. I checked back from time to time, but couldn't live my life at the Lake's edge, in pain and suffering.

The Lake is a large body of water, sometimes filled with tears. It is an emotional holding space and you and your clients can gain much knowledge about depression, sadness, grief, and deep emotional churnings. It can be a space of joy, playfulness, family connections, and watery revelry. Emotions are in motion in the lake. Fluidity is key, so moving stuck energies is very likely, if the client chooses.

The weather is important as well, as is the position of you or your client. Are you on land or in the water? If you are in the water – are you in a small row boat, a jet ski, a sailboat, a yacht? Are you swimming in a tube, a raft, doggy paddling, or drowning?

There is much imagery here that can be moved within the Quantum effortlessly. Movement, then, in 3D quickly catches up and you find your life changes. Things align differently. It's almost like magic. That's one of the beauties and joys of this work! I usually travel to the Lake through another portal than the Sacred Grove.

"Visualize walking through a sweet- smelling forest. Up ahead you are drawn to a special, Ancient Tree and you rest your back against its comforting presence. The Tree feels nurturing, like a mother's embrace. You feel safe and secure."

"As you sit against the trunk, you feel a round knob behind you. As you turn to look, you realize that there is a door hidden in the tree trunk. You turn the knob and the door swings inward. You step within and through the back of the Tree into a lakefront. It could be a small beach leading to a beautiful Lake. It could be a picnic area leading to the Lake. Choose a favorite spot of land near this Lake."

"The Lake is a special place where your Inner Child can play. You notice that you are both your Parent and your Child. The Lake shows your emotions, the fluid give-and- take of your life journey. See yourself. Are you in the water? Are you in a boat? Are you alone? Let yourself rest and get inspiration and healing in this place of Knowledge and Refuge."

"Perhaps Dolphin comes to play with you. Or Whale comes to sing a song that you understand. You know you can swim and play in the water safely and joyfully. Enjoy your time here…"

Inner Child: The Picnic

You can enjoy a Picnic at the Lake. Build in a suggestion that you can come out of the water onto the shore and sit at a picnic table overlooking the Lake. This is a good place to visit with Loved Ones, both incarnated and in Spirit.

> *"Spend some time in a water that feels nourishing and special to you. Perhaps you are playing with waves in the ocean. Or, maybe you are lying on a tube, floating down a river. You enjoy being in water because it is so healing and so inspiring."*

> *"You love to connect with the angelic dolphins and whales who come to play with you. There is a favorite game you have – diving deep together through a rainbow- colored vortex in the middle of the sea."*

> *"You see the rainbow in the water and know the doorway to your special place is within. You take a breath and dive within… and come out to a Picnic ground near the Sacred Lake. You have been here many times and love coming here"*

> *The Lake is a special place where your Inner Child can play. You notice that you are both your Parent and your Inner Child. Perhaps you are five or six years old. This is such a special place to visit!"*

> *"When you are ready, come out of the Lake, onto the shore. Rest and refresh yourself after so much play. You notice there is a Picnic going on around you. So much food and fun! Games, colorful tablecloths, children running around playing."*

"Then you notice you are with Someone who love you so much. They might have passed, but here they are with you now! They are young and healthy and so very happy to see you and to spend this beautiful day with you Picnicking!"

"Enjoy this precious time together. Tell them how much you love them. Listen to their stories and journeys…"

Healers Hall

The Healers Hall is a wonderful place to visit!

This is true, especially for clients who have come for a healing and for those who are receiving an attunement for Reiki 1 and Reiki 2 Practitioner Level.

The Healers Hall is in Quantum, multidimensional, sacred space. It is often also in dream space. I have visited this Hall on a number of occasions in sleep before I brought it forward as a Guided Visualization for others.

I usually start with the Archway of Flowers and then enter from the Sacred Grove.

> *"See yourself walking through a meadow scene on a beautiful day. It is the perfect temperature. You look down and see that you are walking on a path of rainbow colored small stones."*

> *"Up ahead is an Archway of Flowers. You are excited to cross dimensions into the Sacred Grove. As you step underneath the archway, you smell the inviting scent of roses and honeysuckle and hear the soft waterfall in the Sacred Grove. Follow the path to the Waterfall."*

> *"Immediately you see a Being of Love and Light who has come to escort you to the Healer's Hall. You turn and find yourself outside a beautiful hillside temple, the Hall of Healers."*

> *"See yourself being escorted down a long hallway inside the Hall. There are doorways to the left and right of you. You can see through a small window into the rooms. There are Teachers in every room, discussing healing methods to students and other healers."*

> *"They are teaching about the body, how to heal dis-eases naturally, how to live comfortably on the earth plane. There is so much to learn here!"*

"Spend some time, if you wish, in one or more of these rooms with Healing Angels and Light Beings. You might also visit a healing chamber where you can lay down in a beautiful crystal chamber and allow healings to occur for you."

"Whatever you need is provided for you. If you wish to talk and ask questions, do so. If you wish to be silently healed, breathe deeply and allow the healing sounds, colors and vibrations into your cells and organs, into your thoughts and feelings, into your memories and longings."

"Rest here and be healed."

Advanced Sessions: Hall of Healing Masters

Like the Healing Hall, the Hall of Healing Masters is accessed through the Archway, Waterfall, and Sacred Grove. The Grove seems to be the main meeting and greeting place, where we are escorted to various realms. These and the following multidimensional spaces (below) are for advanced trainings and healing sessions.

Visiting the Hall of Healing Masters is a wonderful location for those on a Mastery pathway and can be especially expansive and inviting for those receiving Reiki Master attunement.

> *"See yourself walking through a meadow scene on a beautiful day. The temperature is perfect. You look down and see that you are walking on a path of rainbow colored small stones."*

> *"Up ahead is an Archway of Flowers. You are excited to enter the Sacred Grove. As you step underneath the archway, you smell the inviting scent of roses and jasmine. The birdsong sounds sweeter, the grass looks greener. You hear the soft waterfall sounds in the Sacred Grove."*

> *"Immediately you see a Being of Love and Light who has come to escort you to the Hall of Healing Masters. You are being recognized and honored as a master energy on the planet at this time."*

> *"You are invited to visit rooms of the Masters and spend time with any Master you feel guided to be with. Soon, you know you will be called forth, recognized and honored as a Reiki Master." (pause)*

> *"You hear your name called and you walk into a long hall, filled with Beings of Love and Light, some whom you know for many lifetimes. They are all here for you, to see you and honor you for all the work you are doing in this lifetime."*

> *"You walk down the aisle and up the 3 steps onto a dais. Your name is sounded in the hall. You are robed in a color – see the color*

now. Perhaps your robe has jewels or embroidery or symbols. See your robe now."

"A diadem is put on your head, signifying your status as a master energy on the planet, dedicated to your Lightwork. See the beautiful design, elements and maybe even jewels in your etheric crown."

"You hold out your hand and receive a gift from the Hall of Healing Masters. This gift symbolizes your dedication, integrity, and ability to work within the area of Lightworker. This tool enhances you, your gifts, your service, your work and your entire life."

"Turn and see everyone stand and clap for you! You are recognized and honored for being you!"

"Walk down the 3 steps, down the aisle, and outside the entrance. Stay for a while to greet and be embraced by all the Beloveds who have come to honor you in the Hall of Healing Masters. Know that you are invited back at any time…"

Advanced Sessions: Hall of Records

The Hall of Records is an interesting and specialized multidimensional site. All the knowledge ever accumulated is kept here, in the etheric rings. All of your personal soul journeys, your Akash, is recorded here. The time fractals are located here. It's an amazing location!

You can access it in a number of ways – through the Sacred Grove, through the Hall of Healing Masters, through the Ancient Tree, there are many portals. Here, we are entering through the 6th chakra, the brow chakra.

(Touch the client lightly on the brow chakra.)

> *"See your 6th chakra as a beautiful bluish, purple vortex. As you look within, see a large library. There are high ceilings with rows upon rows of books and instruments, as far up as your eye can see. And, there are ladders right in front of you to climb so you can get the exact information you want."*

> *"There's a fireplace with comfy arm chairs set up just for you. Look out the window onto the large garden and gentle hills, a beautiful scene as far as you can see. It is such a serene, open, expansive and gentle vista."*

> *"You see there is a winding staircase that goes up and up. As you follow it, you notice that the ceiling is rounded, like a dome. You are in the Observatory. A click of the button and the ceiling opens onto the heavens. You can see the stars, galaxies, and cosmos, as much or as little as you would like to see."*

> *"You also realize there are Beings of Love and Light available to sit with you as you research, or to help you find what it is you are looking for."*

> *"There is so much here to see and research! You have time after time after time. Go wherever you wish – to the arm chairs, to the windows, or the books or the observatory."*

" You are welcome here. You are always welcome here! Ask any questions you have, and listen for the answers…"

Advanced Sessions:
DNA Activation Room
DNA Restoration & Rejuvenation

This is an interesting sacred space where a number of activities can occur. An advanced energy healing method, the work done in these rooms are Guided for each client, or for work that you wish done on yourself.

Choose an activity – either DNA Activation or DNA Restoration and Rejuvenation. They are similar but have different component energy methods. DNA Activation allows the DNA to be increased on a scale. Kryon has said that current DNA levels are around 30 - 33%. Masters' and Avatars' levels are closer to 100%. Increasing ours even a little is a major update to our systems and higher order gifts.

DNA Restoration and Rejuvenation involves restoring the etheric template to its optimal functioning. There is also intent that cells, organs, systems all set a pattern of rejuvenation, rather than deterioration. In the work I do and teach, there are elements that we can include to open the door for this work to be done. It is not complete at this time. We are just beginning to work with cellular rejuvenation on an energetic level.

Both of these rooms I was Guided into… and, although not complete, still they are subtly transformative. It is exhilarating to do our work on the leading edge of thought.

I use the Vocal Harmonic songs, Language of Light energy glyphs and advanced healing methods detailed in Books 9, 10, and 11 in the Tools for Lightworkers Series. These include Symphonic Fractals of Light, Spectrum Energetics Etheric Healing, and SoulAnge Harmonics.

"In the Sacred Grove, we step behind the Rainbow Waterfall. Immediately behind, we feel the stone wall, wet with the spray from the waterfall. The combination of the sun and the rainbow waters form interesting patterns on the wall, almost like a wave of liquid light."

"The iridescent wave is mesmerizing, and we follow it with our hands for a few minutes. Incredibly, it seems to materialize as a giant crystal, a very large, convex quartz crystal doorway with waves of light rippling over its surface. It's the Crystal Portal to the DNA Chamber!"

"We step through and are immediately escorted by a Being of Light into a round crystalline chamber. We feel safe and embraced in this beautiful chamber. There is a chair we sit on. The chair feels almost alive, with humming sounds and vibrations echoing from the walls, the ceiling, and the chair. We are being massaged by angelic chords and hymns. These are the very vibrations of the universe!"

"This beautiful Being of Light comes in to talk to us and ask what it is that we want. And why. Why do we want to activate higher?"

"The DNA Activation occurs in the chair. We can just sit and enjoy the process. She asks us what number do we see that we would like to increase our DNA to? Each one number higher from our current setpoint of 33 is exponential. Do you want 34, 35, 36, higher?"

"Relax in this wave of vibrational symphonies…"

Advanced Sessions: Light Grid

This wonderful Guided Visualization is a gift for those of us who identify as Lightworkers. As one who chooses to incarnate to raise the consciousness or light quotient on the planet, we are invited to sit amongst the Spiritual Luminaries who set a Light Grid around this beloved and sometimes beleaguered planet, Gaia.

You are always welcome! There is a space for you!

> *"You meditate and reflect upon the area of light (and the corresponding area of shadow) that you are drawn to in this lifetime. Perhaps it is abandoned children, or animals, or ecosystems. Perhaps it is to help those feeling lack and loneliness, to ascend to abundance and connection. There are so many wonderful areas that you are drawn to. Choose one now."*

> *"As you chose, you feel the air shimmering around you. Your Lightbody, or Merkaba, is expanding. The sound has been made. The call has gone out. Lightworkers around the world, millions of magnificent Souls, throughout eternity, beam Love, Light, Clarity, Compassion, Kindness, and Connection from a pearlescent Light Grid which encircles the globe."*

> *"See yourself, in your Lightbody, ascend to the Grid. There is a space there especially for you! Angels know your name! The Universe sings your story of dedication and devotion. Life after life. Always doing the best you can in every situation."*

> *"Gaia Herself, in all her Glory, shimmers into her Planetary Lightbody. You realize that you can understand her Song. Our Solar Angel, our Sun, shimmers in her Solar Lightbody. You can also understand her Song."*

> *"You look all around you. Here you are, in your Lightbody, sitting with Angels and Bodhisattvas, with Masters and Eternal Qualities. You are joined with a Light Grid which encircles the planet like a*

webbing of pearls. And, you are sending to 'hot spots' or dark areas in the space time fabric which encircles our planet. You are sending to increase the Light Quotient on the planet. You are sending help to those below who are begging for someone, anyone, to hear and to help."

"You are a Lightworker, lighting up. You are so dearly loved and appreciated for doing this work. Enjoy being here in the Light Grid, lighting up. You know you are always welcome. And, always needed."

Design Your Unique Guided Visualization
Step 2: The Journey

You step across the threshold... what do you see, hear, smell? Who do you meet?

Version 1:

Version 2:

Chapter 10

Step Three: The Homecoming

The final step in Guided Visualization is to bring the client back again to their bodies, feeling safe and energized. Clients might have had a strong experience and, perhaps, traveled far! It is our job to bring them back. Don't leave them in multidimensional space.

The easiest way to bring them back is to inform them it is time to leave and then retrace your steps. Also, it's important to remind them that they can go back any time, so the homecoming is not bittersweet or resistant.

Once, in a workshop on channeling, I went very deep within myself. I could hear the workshop leader say it was time to come out, but I felt so deep inside, so warm, so embraced, that I resisted. I heard the woman call my name a few times, with a growing sense of urgency. I wanted to respond and come back to consciousness but felt a frisson of fear that I didn't know how to make my way up again. After another moment of so I followed her suggestions to breathe, to move my hands and feet, to open my eyes. And, immediately, I was back in my body and conscious mind once again.

Talking with the workshop speaker afterwards I voiced a fear - what would happen if I did more of these visualizations and couldn't find my way back home? I would be stuck! She assured me that would never happen. I might fall asleep and wake up as if from a dream. Most likely, I would just move or open my eyes and the journey would be over.

She also assured me that 'guided visualizations' don't go as deep – this was a workshop on full trance channeling that she was offering. As I went so deep, I could be a good candidate to do full trance channeling, she said. (This occurs when a person steps aside, in a sense, and allows another Being of Love and Light to speak through us.)

It was clear to me after that experience that, although fascinated with this form of communion and communication, I did not feel safe handing my consciousness over for even a while. I like to be in my body, awake and aware, to dialogue with Spirit. Which is one reason I am writing this book.

Guided Visualizations are important energy tools for those of us who consciously walk the path as Lightworker. Guided Visualizations are safe, and keep the client secure, grounded as well as open to the quantum doorway that they might, in free will, open and step through. They also have free will choice to visualize another setting. Or, they have free will choice to track the session consciously without journeying anywhere. Or, fall asleep. All choices are acceptable and honored.

Basic Homecoming

Remember to bring your client back from their journey and to ground them back to 3D reality. You also want to suggest that they align with their vitality, feelings of safety, security and groundedness. Working in the etheric planes, which is what we do when we are in Guided Visualizations, can often leave us feeling spacey, woozy, dizzy, and over emotional. They might have had a profound and deep experience visiting with Light Beings or Loved Ones. Crying over the meeting with someone they cherish who has passed is common. Falling into a deep sleep is also common.

For the return journey, bring them gently back into their everyday consciousness and into their body awareness. I usually start with the following suggestions:

"And now, it is time to make our way back from the Healer's Hall (for example). Take your time embracing and being embraced by these Beings who love you so very much. Perhaps one or more of Them walk you back to the Archway of Flowers."

"Know that you are always welcome to visit anytime you want to! This invitation is always there for you. You might make one last embrace, or listen to one last message. Then, under the Archway you go, back to the beautiful meadow, back onto the rainbow rock pathway."

"Back into this room. Back into your body. (pause) Back into your breath. Take 3 conscious breaths, breathing down into your feet, into the earth, feeling your roots going down." (pause as you lightly touch their feet)

"You feel grounded, safe, secure, vital and energized. When you are ready, begin to bring your consciousness back to your eyes, and lightly move your fingers and toes."

"Welcome back!"

And, as I am welcoming them back to their everyday awareness, I also put a Cho Ku Rei on their feet. You can also lightly touch their feet or their arm to make contact and bring bodily awareness. Give them a few minutes to reorient. Then share some of your information, if you feel comfortable doing that.

What information to share, and how to share it, is described in detail in Books 7 and 8 of the *Tools for Lightworkers Series, Reiki 1/ 2, and Master Manuals.*

No Matter the Portal

This sample Homecoming can apply to almost any Earth based Guided Visualizations. If you are going through the knobbed doorway of the Ancient Tree, return them to and through the forest. The same for the Bubble Membrane.

Retrace their steps in the Elevator or Stairs, reversing the process of moving the exact number of flights or steps. If you moved them up to floor 11, then move them back down to level 1. Or, if you are guided to, choose a floor one level above from where they started, indicating that they will now have access to a higher understanding of their life choices. That alone is a blessing for them.

For the advanced, etheric plane journeys to the various Halls, the Healer's Hall, the Hall of Masters, the Hall of Records, the DNA Chamber, and the Light Grid, you can have them move fairly quickly back through the portal and into your room as if they have walked through a secret passageway in *Clue*. You don't always need to take them step by step back.

Follow your intuition about the timing and their return journey.

Regardless of the portal chosen or the exact return journey steps, I always end with:

> *"Back into this room. Back into your body. (pause) Back into your breath. Take 3 conscious breaths, breathing down into your feet, into the earth, feeling your roots going down." (pause as you lightly touch their feet)*

> *"You feel grounded, safe, secure, vital and energized. When you are ready, begin to bring your consciousness back to your eyes, and lightly move your fingers and toes."*

> *"Welcome back!"*

When I say these word to them, I follow the directions myself. I breathe 3 times as I tell them to. I walk to their feet and motion into the earth. I lightly move my fingers and toes to echo the vibratory movements.

You Are Also Coming Back!

You may feel very emotional, humbled, and exhilarated by the journey and the information you have gotten. You may feel exhausted and tired. You need to follow the steps back as well!

And, for both of you, remember to mention drinking water. Energy work changes our vibratory frequency and water allows us to flow more easily into this new state. It replenishes us, almost as if we have taken a physical journey. Have filtered water available for yourself and your client.

Don't schedule another session immediately following. Take some time for yourself to integrate the work you have done.

Below, the Expanded Chakra Meditation, is a unique Guided Visualization that was offered to me in my dreams by a loving Presence of galactic consciousness. You will notice that there are not one but multiple portals, each one individually linked to each of the chakras, starting from 1. Etheric lines or conduits are motioned between each chakra and the corresponding expansion.

The return journey is completed in reverse order, which is common. However, at the end, I was instructed to move back from the 1st up to the 2nd chakra and enfold the entire Visualization in that chakra of Self.

This is an advanced Guided Visualization and I recommend that you do this for yourself, perhaps a number of times, before you offer it to a client. And, again, check in with both your and your client's guidance to be sure this is the correct Visualization for them at this time. Every client has told me it was a very unique and transformative experience.

Expanded Chakra Meditation

"Door Opening

Love Unfolding

Life Unending

On our knees bending"

Breath   *"Take 3 breaths, feeling the comfort and ease with breathing in just the right amount of air, without needing to force or pressure the breath. And feel the relief with breathing out just the right amount without forcing or pushing."*

Ground   *"Now follow your breath down your body, down your legs and out the soles of your feet as if you have roots growing from you. They go down, down into the Earth, as far down as you feel comfortable. And anchor in there – feeling safe, secure, grounded, and protected."*

1st   *"Focus upon your 1st chakra, the root chakra, which is located at the base of your torso. This chakra connects us to safety, security issues, to faith and trust in God and life, and to the lower half of our body. Now expand the connection from your 1st chakra into the core of the Earth, going into the heart of the crystal core center of the Earth, feeling Earth's pulse, her heartbeat, and the strength that comes from this elemental and telluric core. Breathe into this expanded 1st chakra."*

2nd

"*Next, we move up to your 2nd chakra, the relational chakra located just below the navel. The 2nd chakra connects us to our creativity, sexuality, relationships, love, unions and Inner Child. Feel this relational chakra expand to the envelope of skin that surrounds your body. Feel the embrace of the air against your envelope. Now breathe and expand further into your Lightbody, visualizing your aura, mental, emotional, spiritual and energy fields expanding 3 to 6 to 12 feet outwards front and back, left and right, top and bottom. Here you are in your energy state. Breathe into this expanded 2nd chakra.*"

3rd

"*We move up to your 3rd chakra, located at your solar plexus. This chakra connects to the power and control in your life; this chakra is your identity center. Feel the connection with this chakra as we expand to the Gaia partnership, honoring the fullness of incarnating into physicality on Earth. Expand to encompass your home, your state, your country, your continent, and then the entire world. Expand further to the envelope of our atmosphere and a vision of our bejeweled planet spinning in the heavens. Breathe and expand again to include the Earth's magnetosphere, spiraling around our precious planet in protection and angel wings. Finally, connect your 3rd chakra to Earth's complete energy body and auric crown.*"

4th

"We move up to our 4th chakra, our heart center. This chakra connects us to our heart and lungs, breathing life and love into everything we do. This chakra is also related to relationships and unions, to our deepest loves, and also to mercy, compassion, unconditional love and the Bod-dhisatva path. Breathe and expand a connection from your heart chakra to the heart of our Solar Angel, our Sun. Breathe in the warmth, light, and unconditional love from our Solar Angel. Expand further into the heliosphere of our Sun's solar wind and magnetic fields of information. Expand again as the solar influence continues past our planets, past the Kuiper belt, past the Oort cloud, the he-liosheath and into the magnetic sheathing around our magnificent solar system as we spiral, embraced within the Orion Arm. Connect your heart center and 4th chakra to the magnificent solar landscape."

5th

"Move up again to our 5th chakra, our throat center. The 5th chakra connects us to our communications, to speaking our truth and living our truth, living in pristine integrity. Breathe into this chakra and allow an expansive connection from our 5th chakra to the heart of the Mother, our Galactic Mother, the push/pull twin energies at the heart of our Milky Way Galaxy. Feel the connection we have to our Galactic Mother, the Sagittarius A star, and to all energies of hundreds of billions of stars within our magnificent spiraling galaxy as we breathe into our identity of galactic citizen."

6th

"Moving up to our 6th chakra, our brow or 'third eye' chakra connects us to wisdom, knowledge, imagination,

196

intuition and insight. Here we are connected to higher learning, the Hall of Records, higher perceptions and time-less wisdom. We breathe and expand the connection from our brow chakra moving beyond our galaxy and lo-cal stellar neighborhood and beyond the Laniakea Super-cluster and directly into the heart of the Universe, the Fa-ther, the universal matrix grid, a billions of lightyears adven-ture. Here we connect to the heart of the cosmos and our cosmic conscious identity."

7th   *"Door opening."* (Use fingers to widen triangle shape doorway.)

"At the crown of our heads we connect with our 7th chakra, our connection to Source. Breathe through the crown of your head and expand your 7th chakra into the heart of the Multiverse, All There Is, the Central Sun of all the Central Suns. Breathe in this expanded connection and then close the door to a perfect amount."

Encoding   *"Move down from the 7th to the 6th chakra and allow the perfect connection to the Universe. Come back down to the Heart of the Galactic Mother (5th), down to the Heart of our Solar Angel (4th). Back to our Gaia connection (3rd), to our Lightbody (2nd) and all the way to the core of the Earth and our 1st chakra. Feel safe and secure in your rooted Earth energies."*

Enfold

"From the 1st chakra enfold back and anchor into your 2nd chakra, your Lightbody and into your envelope of skin, feeling safe, grounded, vital and serene.

"Door Opening

Love emerging,

life beckoning,

miracles abounding,

life is so astounding,

life unending,

on our knees bending"

… in prayer, dedication and a connected Lightworker identity.

Design Your Unique Guided Visualization
Step 3: The Homecoming

3D is calling you back home.

Version 1:

Version 2:

Vocal Harmonics

Songs for Ending Healing Sessions

Freedom Song

Downpour

We Are Complete

Open Angel Wings

Beacon in the Storm

Freedom Song

ARISE, Sisters, Arise!
Know you are Spirit-Made-Flesh
ARISE, Brothers, Arise!
We are more than our Bio-Mesh

Let Wisdom rise from within
From every cell and every atom
Let Compassion rule your day
Let Mercy be your mainstay
Let Honesty be your guide
From Integrity never hide
Let Knowledge be your shield
Open wide your energy field

ARISE, Brothers, Arise!
Know you are Spirit-Made-Flesh
ARISE, Sisters, Arise!
We are more than our Bio-Mesh

Release fear, pain, anger and grief
Release all your old, stale beliefs
We are eternal, joyful and free
Chose Highest Destiny!
Release what you need to ARISE!
Fly, soar deep inside

ARISE, Sisters, Arise!
We know we are Spirit-Made-Flesh
ARISE, Brothers, Arise!
We know we're more than Bio-Mesh
We know we're more than Bio-Mesh
We are truly Spirit – Made – Flesh
We ARISE in this knowingness

ARISE!

(Note: This song is sung above the client's body. Conduct this song with your arms as you would conduct an Orchestra of Light, rousing courage and clarity.

Downpour

With the downpour of the Healing Flame
The Divine Colors began to rain

Began to reign
Began to reign
Began to reign
Began to reign

With the downpour of the Violet Flame
The iridescent colors spark a manifold game

Began to frame
Began to reclaim
Began to proclaim
Began to reign

With the downpour of the Holy Name
The Divine Colors began to rain

Melody & inspiration for lyrics by Charan Anand

(Notes: This song is sung with hands imitating rain falling down upon the client from head to toe, integrating the healing session. If the Reiki Master symbol, Serpent of Fire, is one you are attuned to, then also put this symbol over the client for gentle integration of healing. Finish with sweeping the client from head to toe.)

We Are Complete

We are complete
We are replete
It is so sweet
Here at your lotus feet
A sweet relief
It is our Heartbeat!

For our sweet Inner Child...
Self-love
Self-acceptance
Self-forgiveness
Self-fulfillment

For (Client's name) of today and always...
Divine unconditional love
Allowing
Embracing
Unfolding
Enjoying

(Notes: The hand symbols for We Are Complete:

1st paragraph: palm open, arms extended over client

2nd paragraph: hands folded over each other at heart center. For each affirmation, ex. Self-love, allow hands to open and pour self-love into the client's field for their Inner Child healing

3rd paragraph: palms open, extended out over client's body. For each affirmation, ex. Allowing, turn hands over and have etheric outpouring into their energy field.)

Open Angel Wings

May (client's name) be at peace
And be a source of Peace in this world

May (client's name) be healed and whole
And be a source of inspiration in this world

May (client's name) be abundant in all ways
And be a source of inner and outer wealth in this world

May (client's name) feel embraced and loved always
And be a source of compassion and connection in this world

OM

HOME

OM

(Notes: For the beginning of each phrase, stand in the middle of the client's body phrase, and put your hands above each shoulder and fluff out their angel wings.

For the second part of each phrase, draw an infinity sign over their body, at the root chakra.

Customize phrases for each client, depending upon what they are working on, and upon your inner guidance.

For each of the ending OM's, raise arms vertically overhead from prayer position, then bring down to your sides, as if you were tracing a large bell. End with hands back in prayer position.

The last OM's are vibrationally toned – allow your body to chime and move in synch with the OM. For example, the 'mmmmm' sound at the end can be held and vibrated as you lower your arms and come back to prayer position. This is a wonderful way to seal in a healing session.)

Beacon in the Storm

There is Hope,
when it seems like hope is gone
There is Peace,
While everything is going on
There is Grace, by your side
And every open door is open wide.

There are days when you want to quit
There are friends who can help a bit
There are songs to lift your heart
There are dreams too large for dreaming
But you have to start

And there is you
The Beacon in the Storm!
If my eyes could see more clearly
Reaching Out for More
There is you
The Lighthouse through the Rain!
Shining light upon me
to bring me home again

In the game that we call life
There is wrong and there is right
I want to rise in spite of all
All I need is to hear your call

Every question has an answer
Every answer has a home
As we figure out together
What we figure out alone

We can really see the future
We can absolutely start
As we stand upon the threshold
Of Our Heart
And, so, we dance
Until the music stops
All of our plans
Take us to the top
But the greatest view that I can see
Is the life we build together,
You and me

And there is you
The Beacon in the Storm!
If my eyes could see more clearly
Reaching Out for More

There is you
The Lighthouse through the Rain!
Shining light upon me
To bring me home again

Music and lyrics by Tony Cardo

Create a Prayer of Intent and Guided Visualization for Your Lightworker Identity

Create a Prayer of Intent and Guided Visualization
for a Global Issue that Calls to You

Create a Prayer of Intent and Guided Visualization for
An Energy Healing Session

Notes and References

Abraham. www.abraham-hicks.comwww.asandra.com

Braden, Gregg. The Science of Miracles, NY: Hay
    House, 2009.

Cardo, Lorelynn Mirage. Lightworker Orientation & Training
    Manual. Portland, OR: Arise Enterprises, 2017.

Cardo, Lorelynn Mirage. Dialogue with Spirit, OR: Arise Enterprises, 2018.

Cardo, Lorelynn Mirage. www.AriseGuide.com

Carroll, Lee. www.kryon.com

Gimbutas, Marija. The Language of the Goddess,
    London: Thames and Hudson, 1989.

Hay, Louise. You Can Heal Your Life. CA: Hay House Inc., 1984.

Kaiser, David. How the Hippies Saved Physics, NY: WW Norton & Co.,
    2011.

Lipton, Bruce. The Biology of Belief, www.brucelipton.com

Radin, Dean. Supernormal, NY: Deepak Chopra Books, 2013.

Schafer, Lothar. Infinite Potential: What Quantum Physics
    Reveals about How We Should Live. NY: Deepak Chopra Books, 2013.

Sheldrake, Rupert, Science Set Free, NY: Deepak
    Chopra Books, 2012.

Sheldrake, Rupert, The Sense of Being Stared At.
    Rochester, VT: Park Street Press, 2013.

Wilcock, David, The Source Field Investigations, NY: Penguin
    Random House, 2011.

Tools for Lightworkers Series

by Lorelynn Mirage Cardo, PhD

Book 1, Daily DeLights Engagement Journal

Book 2, The Mandala of Wholeness: Companion & Compendium for Daily DeLights Engagement Journal

Book 3, Opening Quantum Doorways: Prayer of Intent & Guided Visualizations

Book 4, Dialogue with Spirit: Automatic Writing, Channeled Inspirations, Connecting Within

Book 5, Lightworker Orientation & Training Manual

Book 6, ARISE: A Soul- Based Journey of Counseling & Healing

Book 7, Joining the Global LightGrid: Reiki 1 & 2 Manual

Book 8, Make Today Your Master-peace:
Reiki Master Class Manual
and Daily Engagement Journal

Book 9, Language of Light Fractals:
Advanced Reiki & Healing Energy Glyphs

Book 10, Spectrum Energetics: Manual for Advanced Etheric and Chakra Healing

Book 11, SoulAnge Harmonics: Advanced Energy Healing

Book 12, Chakra Lenses for Careers, Relationships, Health & Joy

About the Author

After following traditional paths of obtaining a master's and doctoral degrees in counseling and education, I followed my heart into the realm of energy healing, bringing these magnificent and subtly powerful perspectives into the counseling, healing and educational fields.

Through the Arise School of Healing Arts, I have incorporated an Apprenticeship Program so those interested in learning or advancing their healing skills can do so within a personal and loving environment. If you are guided to work with me, trust that you are a Lightworker and a Soul-in-Service!

Although I still have my Queens and Long Island, NY, accent, I have been living in Portland, Oregon for many years with my loving family, Tony, Bethany, Parker, and my myriad dogs and cats. Come visit if you are in the area.

The *Tools for Lightworkers Series* is written just for you, from my heart to yours. Let's work together as Lightworkers, shining our light during these turbulent shifting times! As time and distance are not obstacles in our field, connect anytime! Keep in touch with me at Lorelynn@AriseGuide.com or www.AriseGuide.com.

I send Love and Light to you every day. EnJOY!

Acknowledgements

Becoming familiar and adept at both Prayers of Intent and Guided Visualizations will increase your unique intuitive gifts, heighten your healing and energy sessions, and allow you a quick escalator to the heavens within, so you can work from a multidimensional space effortlessly.

Always heartfelt appreciation to one of my personal muses, my soul mate, and twin flame, Tony Cardo. Thanks for all your inspiring lyrics and music! Joy and appreciation to my editor, another personal muse, Bethany Mattson.

Much gratitude and love to my family, my clients, and my Apprentices who inspire me every day to stay connected to Spirit Within. Joely Teller – you opened and held a vision for me of this exact book years ago. Thank you so much for helping me visualize offering these two important Light tools!

I also wish to acknowledge Marni Derr and Chris Duncan from Cue Raven Publishing for formatting, cover design, and artwork. You are the best! And, thanks to Mariana Ruzsak Hollo for your beautiful image of the Conscious Human Tree!

Thanks, and gratitude to Spirit for writing with me all these years and for encouraging me to write this book for you. Thank you, Oriel, for being my writing partner for decades.

www.ingramcontent.com/pod-product-compliance
Lightning Source LLC
Chambersburg PA
CBHW081424090426
42740CB00017B/3177

9 780999 801332